A LITTLE BRIDGE TO HEAVEN

True stories of love, compassion, courage, and faith
from those returning home to God

Tracey Heath, R.N.
Master of Palliative Care

Foreword by Roma Downey

A LITTLE BRIDGE TO HEAVEN
True stories of love, compassion, courage, and faith from those returning home to God

Tracey Heath, R.N.
Master of Palliative Care

Foreword by Roma Downey

Dedicated To

My wonderful Mother & best friend for travelling this path with me.

and

Father Maurice Ward,
My Spiritual Director and Treasured Friend,
"A true Vessel of Our Lady's Love."

Published in 2018 by Modotti Press, an imprint of Connor Court Publishing Pty Ltd

Connor Court Publishing Pty Ltd
PO Box 7257
Redland Bay QLD 4165

sales@connorcourt.com
www.connorcourtpublishing.com.au
Phone 0497 900 685

ISBN: 9781925826081

Front Cover Design: Maria Giordano

Front Cover Picture: Jim Warren

Image of Blue Butterfly: Ronald Hart
Printed in Australia

Note: Except for individuals who gave me permission to tell their stories, details such as names and locations have been changed to protect the personal and medical privacy of the people I write about in this book. The stories are all based on true accounts of my firsthand experience.

Contents

In loving memory of Olga Harmer and Violet Heath,
my angels in heaven.

Three things in human life are important:
The first is to be kind.
The second is to be kind.
The third is to be kind.

Mother Teresa

Acknowledgments

To my wonderful mother to whom I am dedicating this book. For your continual Love, faith and encouragement. How Blessed am I to have you as my mother and Best friend.

Father Maurice Ward, my dear friend and spiritual director, who has been my light in the darkness. Thank you for all your encouragement and support in prayer for all that I attempt to achieve.

Saint Teresa of Calcutta, for her endless compassion, wisdom and faith and being an instrument of God. Giving love to the sick, dying and destitute of Calcutta; for all that she taught me, about caring for the dying and the importance of being of service.

To my friend the beautiful Roma Downey, who has encouraged me from afar to write this book. She has been a great inspiration for me to compose these stories of faith and God's love for those returning home. Thank you Roma for also writing the foreword to my book and being a 'Kindred Spirit' – 'Achieve what I believe'.

My grandmothers Olga and Violet, my angels in heaven for your endless love, encouragement and faith in me and my work; for laying the foundation of my spirituality and loving me for who I am.

A special thanks to all the wonderful patients whom I have had the privilege of nursing, during their final days, for their tremendous faith, trust, courage and love, and the wisdom which they shared.

To the families I have met on this journey. Thank you all for entrusting your loved one to my care and giving me this honour during this sacred time. Thank you also for giving me permission to write their stories.

My heartfelt Thanks and gratitude to my dear friends Dr. Catherine Hamlin (AC), Laura Surdo & Brenda Whitney, for writing their beautiful recommendations for my book. You are all Inspirational women who have dedicated your lives to caring for others.

In loving memory of Maureen Frost, my godmother for being such a special part of my life. Your love of God, the Virgin Mary, Saint Therese combined with a devotion to prayer are a reflection of a life lived in faith.

To my special Aunty Nett, for her continual love, support and wonderful sense of humour. For always believing in me and giving me encouragement. How grateful I am to have you in my life.

To my beautiful cousins Jude and Brian for their love and continual support and being such and important part of my life.

To my close circle of friends especially Jen my best friend for over 35 years. Mary, Penny, Paula, Sarina & Kris for your Love, friendship - living the faith & being true friends.

Sharon my favourite teacher and friend for always believing in me that I would become a nurse, and encouraging me to reach my goals.

To Gwen Bail, the epitome of a real nurse; for being my mentor, giving me the foundation of my nursing career, and teaching me how to give love, compassion and dignity to the aged and dying.

Dina, my friend of many years, you are a wonderful example of compassion, empathy and kindness, and you are a credit to the health care profession.

To Carol for the years of endless typing and friendship.

To artist Jim Warren for granting me permission to use his beautiful painting for the cover of my book.

Jenny Joseph for giving me permission to use her work "Warning".

Finally to my beautiful friends in spirit, who are better known as angels who guide me with my work with the dying and who walk by my side.

Foreword

"There is a time to be born and a time to die."
Ecclesiastes 3:2

Twice in one hundred years a plague brought the mighty Roman Empire to its knees.

As the pandemic spread, the worlds most powerful city wrestled with death and thousands of bodies were piled up in the streets, and people of means fled the city as quickly as possible.

Terror gripped every man, woman and child.

There was an exception among those who could have fled, for the Christian bishops of Rome encouraged their community to stay within the city to pray for the dead and to care for the dying.

In wonderful irony, historians note that this community survived the plague at a much higher rate because of their proximity to the disease as it actually helped them build antibodies against it.

Their compassion was to them a blessing.

The bishops believed it was the responsibility of their community to "weep with those who weep" and to "mourn with those who mourn." They believed that faith was needed the most when men and women "walked through the valley of the shadow of death" and that God was especially present then and there to comfort, to guide and to take their soul from this place to "the place he has prepared."

We all know the inevitability of death, and nearly all of us have struggled to watch a loved one take their final breath. We don't always know how to help in that moment. Now we do, thanks to Tracey Heath.

Tracey takes us on a journey through death – all the while reminding us of the hope we have in Heaven – and along the way she shares with us her wealth of experience as a hospice nurse and how to be a comforter to those we love in their final moments. "A Little Bridge to Heaven" reminds us how we can help bridge the gap between heaven and earth for our loved ones when they need us the most and she reminds us too of the power of prayer.

There is no need to fear. The light is switched off because the dawn has arrived. While death is always painful for those who mourn, Tracey reminds us again and again that without death there is no resurrection.

Roma Downey

Malibu, CA

2015

Beatitudes of the Aged

Blessed are they who understand my faltering step and shaking hand.

Blessed are they who know my ears today must strain to catch the things they say.

Blessed are they who seem to know, that my eyes are dim and my wits are slow. Blessed are they who looked away, when my tea spilled at the table today.

"Blessed are they who never say," You've told that story twice today. Blessed are they who know the ways, to bring back memories of yesterdays.

Blessed are they who make it known, that I'm loved, respected and not alone. Blessed are they who ease the days on my Journey Home, in loving ways.

Ester Mary Walker

1

Hearing God's Call

Life is an amazing mystery, and who better to remind us than the dying?

Ever since I can remember I have known that my life's work was in caring for the aged and the dying. My first experience of this occurred when I was only 12 years of age and on work experience at a local nursing home. During this period I had been assisting to care for Elsie a beautiful old lady, 88 years of age, who was dying of metastatic bowel cancer. I developed a very special bond with this dear old soul. She had only one daughter whom she did not see due to a family dispute. There was a real sadness in her eyes when she spoke of her daughter and it was clear that she loved her dearly, but pride stopped her from making contact. After a great deal of soul searching and prayer she requested that her daughter be phoned to come and see her before she died. "I cannot go to heaven with anger in my heart or without love".

Remarkably, the daughter responded to the summons immediately. In that brief window of opportunity proceeding Elsie's imminent death, they made their peace. They spent hours reminiscing about old times, laughing and crying, but most importantly giving each other the love they both so desperately wanted.

As I entered the room there was an amazing feeling of peace and tranquility. It seemed to me like the very presence of God. As both mother and daughter embraced joyfully, for what would soon be the last time, their eyes sparkled with pure Love. Not wanting to intrude,

I slipped out of the room after instructing them to push the buzzer if they required assistance.

Within ten minutes the buzzer sounded. Elsie had died peacefully in her daughter's arms. Her daughter looked at me with tears in her eyes. "Mum said to tell you that her heart is only full of love, and that you would know what she meant." The Nurse in charge gently placed her arm around me and asked me if I wanted to assist her in washing and re-dressing the deceased in accordance with her daughter's wishes. As I helped, I felt enveloped by the serenity in that room, and at that exact moment I knew my life's calling was to work with the aged and dying.

~

Let there be peace on Earth and let it begin with me.

Jill Jackson & Sy Miller (1995)

~

How Hospice Developed

Our aging populations worldwide mean that more people than ever before are living longer than preceding generations. Although the roots of the hospice movement began in the middle ages with places of "hospitality" providing food and shelter for ill and weary travellers, it wasn't galvanized until the twentieth century, which saw the steepest shift toward an aging populations as increasing longevity rates met decreasing fertility rates.

In the mid-twentieth century, a nurse and social worker turned medical doctor, Dame Cicely Saunders, focused on the unique physical and spiritual needs of the dying, especially in the area of caring for patients who could no longer be cured. These needs were largely unacknowledged and unaddressed by the medical community, in which anything short of curing was considered failure. Saunders' pioneering work founded the first hospice, St. Christopher's, in the

UK, but she lectured abroad and her palliative techniques quickly spread. Within a few years Elisabeth Kübler-Ross published her ground-breaking work on the stages of grief, *On Death and Dying,* and the modern hospice and palliative care movement was fully in gear.

Where I grew up in Australia, hospice work began to take off late in the twentieth century with a "live until you die" focus on providing residential care for the aged. But anyone familiar with Western medicine knows that hospice care often runs counter to prevailing professional practices and cultural norms.

For many, the topic of death and dying is distasteful or even frightening. Doctors and nurses are not necessarily taught how to discuss these topics with patients and their families. Even in aged-care settings, we might hear the usual daily questions, "Has the resident/ patient received morning medication, pain management? Has personal hygiene been completed? Palliative Care plan adhered to?" But rarely will we hear, "Has the resident/patient been asked about his or her spiritual needs? Has his or her spirit been attended to?"

Spiritual Gifts Go Both Ways

Of course these questions matter greatly for patients. But they are concern for both the caregivers attending to them and for their loved ones. Here is the secret that hospice workers already known, end of life care/ Palliative Care is a holistic model of care which incorporates Body, mind and Spirit. When our precious loved ones are dying, we need help from others who have gone through it and can help us prepare—for the gifts we can give, and for the gifts we can receive.

You will read about my beloved friend Father Paddy, who gave me the image of "A little bridge to heaven." There will be language in this book about heaven, and God, and angels. My language comes from my Catholic faith, but God is not bound by it. I invite you to sift through my experiences and glean what is helpful to you, regardless of your own background or present convictions.

Like no other topic, death and dying compel us to think of what lies beyond that uncertain horizon. My purpose is not to try to convince you to believe what I believe. My purpose is to give you comfort, hope, and confidence that there are amazing spiritual gifts, unique to the dying process, which can be exchanged between people—whether family, loved ones, or bedside strangers—and to encourage you to seek them out. And to Gently introduce you to the possibility of God, Faith, Prayer and Grace.

So I use the phrase "a little bridge to heaven" to help you picture yourself as a friend to the aged and dying, helping them cross from this life to whatever they sense awaits them on the other side. Death is a transition, even for those who believe it to be the end. You too can become a little bridge just when it is needed.

But a bridge is made to connect two bodies of land on either side of a canyon or body of water, isn't it? Traffic across it usually goes both ways. Those of us who have received gifts from the dying know that we are standing on holy ground. If you are facing the death of a loved one, it may well be that they will become *your* bridge to heaven in giving you a glimpse of something wonderful you could not otherwise have seen.

Glimpsing the Beyond

My faith gives me ways of understanding the dying process in the context of an eternal life that I believe includes, yet exists beyond, this earthly plain. However, had I not been raised with a faith, my experiences in accompanying and caring for the terminally ill have made it extremely clear to me that they on a final journey home to Somewhere or Someone. In end of life care patient's spiritual needs are just as imperative as the physical. Symptom control is important not just to ease suffering, but to empower the dying to do the work that only they can do. Death can happen suddenly, shockingly, but for most of us, the dying process is labor.

The dying process need not be a labor of fear. It can be a labor of love. There are spiritual gifts waiting for us as well as for our cherished loved ones.

So I offer you these stories to help dispel fear so that it might give way to the power of love. As a palliative care nurse, I carry the last glances of many patients in my heart, special people who have touched my life in the most extraordinary ways, all of whom have played a significant part in my own spiritual journey. I hope they will help you recognize and be grateful for your own journey through life at precisely those times when death leaves its marks on you. Those marks may feel like wounds, but in the great mystery of our life in God they are also gifts. Try as we might, we cannot disentangle pain from love, or tears from laughter.

Take a Few Steps

This book comprises some of my favourite stories about those facing their final journey home to God. It has taken shape from insights of faith, hope, love, wisdom, and courage. I have selected experiences from around the world, not just about the dying but about others I have been privileged to work alongside. Their humble service to humanity has been an inspiration to me and has helped me on the path of my own spiritual journey.

Naturally, I hope to help nurses, doctors, and other healthcare professionals to become more open to the wonder and awe of human spirit in their care for the sick and dying. I also hope that these stories give those just commencing their nursing careers something to ponder on, to give them more insight into the dying process and the importance of caring for the Human Spirit in end of life care.

I would also like to assist all those who are facing the death of a loved one, or who are still wrestling with their experience of the death of a loved one, to see this process as a opportunity for spiritual gifts to be given as well as received. In the profession we speak of being "invited" by the dying to accompany them on their final journey. This is a time of deep listening, reflection, and exploring existential questions. For the one dying there is no "dress rehearsal", this creates a sacred space for sharing, without restriction, a time that becomes pure and from the heart.

Will you take a few steps with me in this book across the great divide between what we know and what we don't know? Don't be anxious about the strangeness that may surround these stories. It is not uncommon for the dying to have what we would call "mystical" experiences—to see Jesus, Virgin Mary, Angels, white light, smell fragrant aromas, to hear voices of loved ones to reach out and try to touch something or someone unseen. This combined with an "inner, knowing" of their own death and synchronicity of events appears to be common occurrences. I believe it is because the dying are given a glimpse of heaven, while still on this earthy plane, it is although they have already commenced their heavenly transition and have been given a sneak peak of what awaits them in the next dimension. We do not have to understand these experiences in order to be grateful for them.

But if these mystical experiences do not happen when we lose a loved one, or if the dying experience was largely negative, neither do we have to feel confused and worried. Knowing how others experience the dying process may give us tremendous comfort, insight, and knowledge in helping us process our own stories in the perspectives of others'. Ultimately we are all struggling with things that will forever be shrouded in uncertainty, but we can help lift the veil for each other. We can become "little bridges to heaven" for one another in this earthly journey, from ignorance to understanding, from trauma to healing, from fear to peace.

Sometimes families will confess to me, "I don't know what to say," or "I'm afraid to go into the room, what can I do?." These anxieties, fears and insecurities are normal. And they can fade quickly with just a few simple steps of practical advice, by encouraging families to become involved in their loved ones care in simple non threatening ways, such as holding of a hand, assisting with a sponge bath, or quiet gentle listening.

Simply being present in silence is far more powerful than most of us would think. Healthcare professionals speak of listening to what patients "mean," not just what they say. I believe that silence is a way of making room for the spirit for both the dying and the loved one to just "be", in that sacred space. Providing the opportunity for the dying to ponder on their own meaning and purpose of their lives, and what really matters from the heart – it may also open the channels for tremendous healing, forgiveness and love through caring and honest communication.

The human body on earth is forever changing through its cycles of life—if we are fortunate, from infancy, to youth, to adulthood, and finally to old age. I believe that when we die, all that remains visible to the naked eye is an empty shell, which we used while on earth. Our human spirit returns to that dimension of connecting directly with God.

When we die, both the Spirit and the Physical Body Surrender. Even if you are not sure what you do or don't believe about God, body, spirit, soul, heaven or afterlife, you will need your own safe, sacred space and the comfort of others around you while dealing with the transition of a loved one.

In the meantime, you have the stories of others. How will they teach you to be kind and caring and compassionate for yourself and others? In what ways will you discover how to facilitate caring for a loved ones "Spirit" and assist them to discover meaning as they look back on their lives? Let's learn together.

~

I regard the Aged as Travellers who
Have gone on a Journey which I too may have to go,
Of whom I ought to Inquire whether the way is smooth and easy Or
Rugged and Difficult at times.

Socrates

~

2

Father Paddy: "A Little Bridge to Heaven"

Medjugorje in Bosnia Herzegovina is considered a very sacred place by many people throughout the world. During my visit there I met some wonderful people, all with their own stories to share of their own unique spiritual journey. Travellers from all over the world would flock to Medjugorje, searching for inner peace and, I imagine, a validation of their faith.

The spiritual energy was extremely strong with prayer, adoration and worship, and there was also a tremendous sense of connection with strangers.

It was through confession that I met a wonderful Catholic priest – 87 years of age – Father Paddy. He sat quietly outside St James church, on an old wooden chair, patiently waiting to hear the confessions of pilgrims passing by. His piercing blue eyes, shining brightly in the sunshine, and his warm and loving smile captured my attention immediately. Our eyes met and he gestured for me to sit down. As I approached I could clearly sense that there was something extremely special about this old man.

As we began to speak it became obvious to me that I was not there for Confession but to listen to Father Paddy's story. I sat quietly listening as he spoke about his life's vocation into the priesthood, his frail hands gesturing when he wanted to make a point. Those old hands, which had ministered to hundreds over the years, had blessed so many, and had held the hand of someone when they were dying. "We know that story telling begins in the heart, when the heart opens grace enters". Roma Downey.

He spoke of his life's vocation – calling into the priesthood and the sacrifices he made to enter the ministry, but there was no regret. He was so humble and thankful to God for the full life that he had led, for the people he had loved, and those who had loved him. For the strangers who became friends and those whom he had ministered to over the years … they were all part of his tremendous journey through a life which he considered blessed.

He had given his life to serve God from a very early age, and had a great passion for ministering to the dying, 'to assist souls to heaven'.

He spoke of faith, love and hope, death and the privilege of caring for those in their final days. We discussed my work, we laughed, and even cried at some of the stories we shared about the human spirit, and the courage and faith of those who had crossed our paths. I also spoke of my devotion to Saint Therese, and told Father Paddy about the variety of rose petals which would appear 'out of nowhere', often after or during the period of when I was caring for the dying. He assured me that each petal was a visit from the Blessed Saint Therese.

Father Paddy also spoke of his other passion, which was teaching. He had taught in Catholic schools for many years in Ireland, and was particularly fond of the 'youngsters', as they had given him such joy and purpose in his life over the years. He explained with great emotion that just because he was a priest it was assumed that he had it 'all together', and did not need to speak of his life, his anxieties and fears. It was not long into the conversation that Father Paddy shared with me that he had advanced bowel cancer which had metastasised to his liver, and he was in Medjugorje for the very last time. He appeared to have a deep insight into his own death, stating that he would be 'going home' very soon. He confidently stated that he would die in Medjugorje.

There was no anger, no fear, just acceptance. He spoke of dying as returning home to God and all those who he loved, and the joy of such a reunion. There was only one more event which Father Paddy longed to see once more before he died and that was the mystery of the 'dancing sun'.

He described these breathtaking phenomena as supernatural, not of this world, but a gift from God. The brilliance of the dazzling orange sun, as it would literally dance off the mountain tops in splendour. The light so dazzling, that one could only witness this magnificence for short periods. This was considered a heavenly wonder, and one which many pilgrims to Medjugorje had witnessed. How he longed to see this heavenly vision once more.

When I stood up to leave, after conversing for many hours, Father Paddy embraced me, kissing me on the cheek and softly whispering into my ear, 'Continue to be a little bridge to heaven, my little darling. Thank you for listening; nothing is by chance, my love. God takes you where you need to be. Always continue to listen, and follow and to serve all those who are dying, with love, compassion and dignity – and nurture the spirit within each individual … For it is the human spirit which leads a soul home to the almighty. God Bless you.'

On the way back to the hotel, I could not help but feel that I had left a treasured friend, there had been a real soul connection, and I felt extremely blessed to have met this beautiful priest.

∼

"Some people come into our lives and quickly go. Some people move our souls to dance. They awaken us to a new understanding with the passing whisper of their wisdom. Some people make the sky more beautiful to gaze upon. They stay in our lives for a while, leave footprints on our hearts, and we are never, ever the same."

Flavia Weedn.

∼

Later I met some friends and we sat outside in a small cafe. The night was warm and still, and there was a real sense of serenity as we sat and quietly sipped our coffee. While contemplating my encounter with Father Paddy, I just happened to glance up into the night sky towards the mountains. The bright orange sun was setting, and appeared to be dancing, pulsating happily on the top of the mountain, just like Father Paddy had described to me. It was magnificent, the brightness of the sun almost made it too difficult to look at with the naked eye. The sky was lit up with magnificent luminous bright orange light. I had never seen anything so beautiful in my life. It was a true gift of the divine. I prayed that dear Father Paddy had also witnessed the radiance of the dancing sun.

Early the next morning I was visited by one of Father Paddy's friends who informed me that Father Paddy had also witnessed the dancing sun. He had stated to his friend that it was a true gift from God and was overcome with emotion at such magnificence. He was now ready to go home, closing his eyes for the last time, dying peacefully, that night, in his beloved Medjugorje.

When I opened my Journal to write about Father Paddy, there was a red rose petal—and ever so faintly but distinctly, an image of Saint Therese upon it.

~

Only a life lived in service to others is worth living.
Albert Einstein

~

3

Olga's Story: People Get Ready

My beautiful grandparents have played an intrinsic part in the development of my spiritual beliefs and values. Both my grandmothers were extremely 'spiritual', and possessed a deep faith. I shared a very close and unique spiritual relationship with both of these women. We could sit for hours and talk about God, life, death and supernatural phenomena. My mother's mother in particular had some amazing spiritual experiences throughout her life. Some would even say 'supernatural'. This particular Nan and I were very connected on a spiritual level, to the extent that I would know when she was in trouble and vice versa, even from the other side of the world.

Once, while I was in India with an Australian Aid organisation, I had a strong sense that something was wrong with Nan – that strong nagging inner knowing that continues to persist until you act on it. I tried to phone Australia but because of the connections from India could not get through. Therefore, my friend and I sat and prayed for her for many hours as that was all I could do. Often when I am praying deeply, I see a beautiful indigo light, which appears to flood all over me.

The next morning, after being restless all night, I managed to phone Australia and much to my surprise, Nan answered the phone. The first words which she said to me were, 'Thank you for the prayers and the beautiful blue light, I was flooded with it, and at the time I was in hospital as I had a severe angina attack,' Nan had many experiences like this. Another time, I was at work, and told the director of nursing I had to leave and go to my Nan's. She asked why, and all I could say is that she needs help. When I arrived at Nan's home, I was astonished to find fire engines all down the road, as the fuse box attached to her house had caught on fire and subsequently her home was ablaze. My cousin, who lived next door, went over to give Nan her morning paper and, seeing the flames, acted quickly. Thanks be to God!

Nan and I would sit for hours and talk about God, the angels, saints, and heaven. She had a deep faith and one which she practised on a daily basis. We would often jest that she would wear her little knees out praying for all her family. I believe that she had a direct line to heaven, her prayers were extremely strong, and the faith behind them steadfast.

~

Faith is a knowledge within the heart, beyond the reach of proof.
Khalil Gibran

~

Although she was not Catholic, Nan also had a great devotion to the Virgin Mary, and considered her a treasured friend. She believed in angels, and had many mystical experiences where she saw angels in her home.

Nan lived with my parents and me for the last few months of her life and this was a time of many blessings. As her condition deteriorated, Nan was admitted to hospital as she needed further tests. I could clearly see in her old eyes that she was dying. We used to have an agreement between us that she could not die until we said she could, as the thought of her dying was too difficult for me to comprehend.

On Christmas day Mum and I went into the hospital to spend precious time with Nan. That night I had the overwhelming sense to go back. When I arrived I found Nan sitting on the bed crying, I sat hugging her as she said to me, 'I cannot do this anymore.' We spoke of her going to heaven and, even though it broke my heart, I knew that she was getting ready to go. I know that often loved ones need permission before they can depart. I stayed for a long time, she promised that she would not die that night, so trusting Nan's intuition I left and returned home. The next day Mum and I returned to the hospital, Nan was so tired, we had a lovely time with her, and the hospital staff practically ordered us to go home and have a rest. As we left the last thing that I said to Nan was 'I love you'; she gently nodded. Usually she would say it back, but she was so tired, she could not even answer.

As Mum and I sat having a cuppa I said, 'Do you know that Human Nature song 'People get ready'? There's a train a-coming, don't need no ticket to climb on board, all you need is faith? I think Nan is on that train.' Just as the words came out of my mouth the hospital phoned to tell us that Nan, after finishing a glass of lemonade, closed her eyes and quietly boarded the train of light.

We were both devastated. When we arrived at the hospital, I asked if I could please attend to my Nan with her final wash. As the hospital staff knew me, they let me do so. Mum assisted me with this, and it was one of the most beautiful privileges of our lives. Once again the three of us were in the room together for the last time. Nan's face was that of an angel, a gentle smile on her lips, and a look of surprise as though she had met an old friend. In our hearts we knew that she was in heaven, surrounded by more love than is humanly imaginable.

Nan had a small Bible which she always wanted me to have. A few weeks after she had died, I had a beautiful dream about her; it was very real. Nan was telling me to go up to the small cupboard in her home as there was something waiting there for me. When I asked Mum, she replied that all had been cleaned out of the cupboard and there was nothing there. As my dream was so clear, and Nan was so insistent, I asked to go up to look for myself.

As I approached the old small brown cupboard, all the wonderful memories of my childhood came flooding back. For me that cupboard had contained all the magical treasures of Nan's life. As a young child we would spend time, looking in her brown leather music box at all her jewels, and she would tell me the amazing stories behind each piece. This was an activity which I loved to share with Nan; it was like looking in a treasure chest. When opening the cupboard, I would immediately be hit with the refreshing perfume of camphor balls. Nighties, usually blue or pink, would be carefully packed on the top shelf and undergarments in the one below. In several other shelves were the treasures, beautiful golden gloves, wonderful books, drawings and cards which I had given her when I was a young child, several of her cardigans which all had the aroma of *Charlie* perfume, various pieces of magnificent jewellery – sparkling brooches, earrings and necklaces.

My mind drifted back to the present moment. This time as I opened the old cupboard door, there was nothing – no camphor, no aroma of *Charlie* perfume, no real evidence that Nan had even really been there. I felt so sad as I missed her so much. Just as I was about to close the door to the cupboard, the sunshine reflected onto something gold in the corner. I bent down, and under a piece of contact, was the small Bible which Nan had always wanted me to have. The gold which had caught my attention reflecting in the light was the sign of healing, which many medical personnel have on their Bibles.

Since Nan died, I have had many spiritual experiences, where I have felt her presence, and I know that she is watching over us always and is indeed my guardian angel.

~

"I have an Guardian Angel in Heaven, I call her Nan"

Tracey Heath 2018

~

4

Frosty: Angel of God

How often in my work over the years I have explained to countless families that sometimes we are not meant to be with our loved one when they die. Very often it is not until the family member leaves the room momentarily the person dying can 'let go'. I believe that the bond of love shared between the one dying and the family is often so strong that the person dying cannot do so until the family member leaves the room, giving permission for that bond to be broken.

It may be that a family member does not get to their loved one's side in time, perhaps the traffic was bad, perhaps they stopped for a cup of coffee, or the flight was delayed. But for whatever reason, they arrived just after the person had died. Of course one goes through the 'what if', 'what if I had caught a cab', 'what if I did not stop for that coffee', 'what if I had changed the flight'. But maybe this was meant to be God's plan. Sometimes we do not get to physically say goodbye. We all come into this world surrounded by God's love and depart the same way, at the exact moment that we are meant to return home to our creator. I believe that we are all just a soul having an earthly experience, and that when we die the spirit goes on. The empty shell which is the body is only a vessel for our time here on earth. So even though we may anticipate being present for a loved one's death, God may have different ideas.

This was to be the case for my beautiful godmother. Maureen (Frosty) was of Irish decent and in her early 60s when our paths first crossed. We met over 13 years ago when I was working at an aged care facility waiting to complete my bachelor degree. We had an immediate connection. I believe that it was a soul connection, and for the next 13 years a very special friendship developed.

She was a frail little lady, only 5 feet tall; her body was very crippled with osteoarthritis, which meant that her only way of getting around was with the aid of a large walking frame. Maureen was a very pretty lady; she had beautiful piercing blue eyes, and porcelain skin. Mentally, she was as sharp as a tack, thus making it difficult to live in a facility with other residents who had dementia and were unable to communicate. She coped with a great deal over the years and it was her tremendous faith that always shone through in adversity.

Frosty would love to sit for hours talking about God, angels, Our Lady, life, death and the wonder of the human spirit. And of course her beloved St. Therese. When we first met she gave me a small picture of the beautiful little saint in a frame, and this picture was, for me, the catalyst and introduction to both the Catholic faith and this special saint. Every morning before having breakfast she would, without fail, pray to the little flower asking her to guide me with my work with the dying and to be with me always. Saint Therese became a mutual friend to the two of us.

~

I will spend my heaven doing good upon earth.
Saint Therese, (1873 – 1897)

~

I believe Maureen had a direct line to heaven, her prayers were extremely strong, pure and from the heart. She had the conviction that her prayers would be heard and answered. How often she would state that without her faith she would not be able to survive. Maureen also taught me 'Oh angel of God', a very special Catholic prayer which would play a very significant part in my own conversion to Catholicism.

Frosty's favourite colour was purple, and so was mine, hence the nickname 'The purple lady'. Over the years she had collected various gifts from all over the world that I had given her from my travels – all the colour of choice; these were displayed with pride on a small stand in the corner of her bed room. She also enjoyed a glass of Bailey's Irish Cream and considered this a real treat, saying that it was the Irish blood in her which made her enjoy a wee nip. 'Hold the ice!'

Christmas Eve, was always a special time. Each year it was a tradition that I would go to the facility with a picnic basket of goodies with all her favourites – mince pies, neenish tarts, rum balls, and of course Bailey's Irish Cream. There was always a glass or two of Baileys shared as we would sit together and watch Carols by Candlelight on the TV.

My how she loved that Baileys! Over the years her desire for Baileys had caused some commotions. Once after consuming two small glasses of Baileys, Frosty left her bedroom to be taken to the bathroom. When she returned to her room, she saw a man climbing out her bedroom window. Quickly she pushed her buzzer for assistance, but by the time the staff had come, he was long gone, and they put it down 'to much Baileys'. 'I am telling you what happened', she stated, 'It was not the Baileys'. Feeling anxious, Frosty phoned me and I came in and sat with her for a few hours until her fear subsided. During that time a man was caught trying to get into another resident's bedroom.

On Christmas Eve 2009, after returning from an overseas trip to Europe, I gathered all the gifts which I had brought for Frosty and our usual assortment of Christmas treats, which we would devour while watching the Carols. Just as I was about to leave, something told me to phone her to say that I was on the way. Instead of my beautiful Godmother's voice, an extremely rude nurse told me in no uncertain terms, 'She is dead'. I was devastated and lost for words. Even though the staff knew me, no-one would give me any information on what had transpired. They were as cold as ice, no compassion, and just did not care; they certainly lacked professionalism. I was disgusted.

Through my network of acquaintances, I tracked down the funeral directors, and as fate would have it, it was the company where I had worked for a period of time when I was undertaking grief counselling. I spoke to the most beautiful woman, Katie (pseudonym), who told me as much as she could without breaking confidentiality. Before long Katie disclosed to me that her father had recently died unexpectedly, and this gave me the opportunity to try to return the compassion and comfort. On reflection we were entwined with our own personal grief.

Frosty had died suddenly and unexpectedly – there was no warning, one minute she was there and the next she was gone. How quickly life can be over! I had no closure, no opportunity to say goodbye, I was beside myself with grief. Before hanging up the phone to Katie, she said to me in such an angelic voice, 'Tomorrow is Christmas Day, a day of blessings, I am sure that she will let you know that she is okay and resting in the palm of God's hand'.

Christmas Day was probably the worst one which I have ever experienced. My grief was so overwhelming; I did not know how I was going to get through the day, even with my family. I could not think, or even pray; I was numb. Then the most amazing event occurred. My brother, the macho motor mechanic, arrived with my two nephews. He was carrying a large parcel carefully wrapped in brown paper. My brother is by no means religious, although he does have a quiet spirituality which he would never admit. He handed me the parcel explaining to me that he did not know who or what this was but he felt that he had to buy it for me. As I unwrapped the parcel I was astounded to uncover the most exquisite statue of Saint Therese, the Little Flower. In that instance I knew that all was well with my darling Frosty and that indeed she was 'resting in the palm of God's hand'. Yet, somehow this had been orchestrated through God's grace for my brother to be used as the vessel to deliver such as beautiful gift. The same gift which joined Frosty and I over 13 years ago, was now being used to bring me comfort, love, and to say goodbye.

~

Angel of God, my guardian dear,
To whom his love commits me here,
Ever this day, be at my side,
To light and guard, to rule and guide'.
Amen

Common Catholic Prayer

~

Warning

When I am an old woman I shall wear Purple,

With a red hat which doesn't go, and doesn't suit me.

And I shall spend my pension on brandy and summer
gloves,

And satin sandals, and say we've no money for butter.
I shall sit down on the pavement when I'm tired,
And gobble up samples in shops and press alarm bells,
And run my stick along the public railings,

And make up for the sobriety of my youth.
I shall go out in my slippers in the rain,

And pick the flowers in other people's gardens,
And learn to spit.

You can wear terrible shirts and grow more fat,
And eat three pounds of sausages at a go,
or only bread and pickle for a week.
And hoard pens and pencils and beer mats and things in
boxes.

But now we must have clothes that keep us dry,

And pay our rent and not swear in the street.

And set a good example for the children,

We must have friends to dinner and read the papers.
But maybe I ought to practise a little now?

So people who know me are not too shocked and
surprised,

When suddenly when I am old, and start to wear purple

Jenny Joseph (Permission obtained 2013)

5

Francesco Luminosità: The Light Is Beautiful

Francesco was an Italian gentleman, 90 years of age, who had been diagnosed with aggressive bowel cancer that had also metastasised to many other organs. He lived at home with Maria, his wife of 60 years. They had nine children, and 11 great grandchildren, and were an extremely close-knit family. Francesco, supported by his family, had made the decision that he wanted to die at home, surrounded by familiarity and his family, rather than the coldness of a sterile hospital room. He was a delightful old man, but could only speak a little English, as Italian was his first language. But we made by just fine.

Being Italian, he was also a devout Catholic, his bedroom was decorated with various Catholic statues and pictures. A small statue of Jesus and the Virgin Mary on his dressing table, while a gold crucifix hung over the bed. His rosary beads were never out of his old hands. He received so much comfort from those rosary beads, and also from daily visits from his local Parish priest. Prayer and worship were both extremely important to Francesco; all the family had a very strong faith. Francesco was aware that he was dying, even though the subject had not really been broached by the family; even with their faith, death was not a topic for conversation. One day, when it was just the two of us in the room alone, he quietly took my hand, looking deep into my eyes and said very clearly 'Paradiso', (heaven), pointing upwards with his hands, 'luminosità, uminosityà', he once again gestured with his hands as to demonstrate everywhere. I knew enough of the Italian language to know that he was talking about the

'Light'. 'Is it beautiful?', I asked. 'Aggettivo magnifico' (magnificent). His whole face lit up when he spoke of the light, there was a real spark back into his old eyes, a kind of knowing and an excitement to share with his family about his own little glimpse of heaven.

This time was a beautiful moment shared between husband and wife, and one in which Francesco was able to speak to his wife from the heart about dying. From that moment on, the family began to speak more openly to Francesco. The next day when I came to nurse Francesco he spoke of 'angelos' (angels) who had visited him during the night, but he could hardly find the words in either English or Italian to describe their beauty 'luminosità, uminosityà'.

As the day progressed Francesco's condition deteriorated, and he became semiconscious. After having the family priest to administer the last rites and pray for Francesco, Maria and her family decided to go and have a sleep. They requested me to wake them if he deteriorated further. I gently explained to his wife that there may not be time to get her and the other members of the family as Francesco was getting very close to dying. I also explained to her that because the bond of love is so strong between the family and the one dying, that it is often only when the family step out from the room for a short period that the person dying can 'let go'. But surprisingly, they still insisted on going for a rest.

As I sat holding Francesco's hand, I spoke gently to him. 'Please let me know when you are ready to go, so that I can call your family back in time, as they really want to be present.' Even though he was drifting in and out of consciousness, he slowly nodded his head. I have always believed that hearing is the last sense to go when one is dying, and always encourage families to speak to their loved ones until they die.

An hour passed, and suddenly he opened his weary eyes and looked towards the corner of the room, 'Beata vergine Maria, Beata vergine

Maria'. With this I got up from my chair, requesting Francesco to 'hold on until I get your family'. Waking all his family, they all came and sat with him, once again he nodded gently and then he was gone.

As I left the family to have some special time with the deceased, I walked up the corridor, and in seeing a picture of the Virgin Mary, I just shook my head and said, 'Gosh, you cut it fine that time', and smiled to myself.

~

> There are two ways of spreading light; to be
> the candle or the mirror that reflects it.
> ~Edith Wharton

~

6

Violet: "I Believe in Angels"

As I write this story about my grandmother, my heart is full of love, and I cannot help but smile as I reflect on this amazing woman whom I had the privilege of calling 'Nan'.

Violet Lucy Bell was 94 years of age when she died. She had been a devoted wife, mother, sister, friend and, more importantly, my grandmother.

I had shared an extremely close bond with this beautiful soul all my life, I was truly blessed. As a child I would stay with Nan and Pa for countless weekends and school holidays, and these visits continued throughout adulthood.

Nan had the most wonderful sense of humour, and was quite mischievous. Sometimes one would get worried what she was going to say next; if she could make you laugh, then she was happy. She was a pure soul, her heart was full of love, she gave as much as she received – if one had Violet in their lives they were blessed.

Nan continued to live independently for many years after my grandfather died. She possessed great courage, and determination and at times was very stubborn. It was these qualities that assisted her to stay in her own home supported by my aunty for many years.

She was always a giver, lending a hand to others in need. She had always wanted to become a nurse when she was a little girl, but because of her circumstances was unable to fulfill this dream. Her mother died when she was only two years of age, and her much-loved father when she was only 16 years old. Her father died at work and

Nan would always remember the vision of him as they brought his body home on a dray. She had one sister who looked after her. She also spent a lot of time in a foster home where she was not treated well. Nan was a very pretty young girl, with a beautiful heart, so was the target of a lot of jealousy from her stepsister and stepbrother. Eventually her older sister took charge and Nan was raised by her, leaving the foster home.

Nan was involved in many community activities such as being life governor at one of Melbourne's largest hospitals and also of the Australian Red Cross (Victoria). She loved her garden and was well known for her beautiful roses – pink, red, apricot and, my favourite, yellow. Each season the garden would be magnificent, with hundreds of roses dancing gently in the breeze. The scent from them was exquisite, they were perfectly formed and looked like no human hand had ever touched them – they were her pride and joy. Nan's love of roses lasted her whole life. She would get such enjoyment from watching a new bud blooming. All the family loved to take home roses from her garden.

~

Lovely flowers are the smiles of God's goodness.

William Wilberforce

~

Nan was a character, to say the least, and would amaze us all with some of her antics. One day, after locking herself out of her house, she decided to climb in through the bathroom window. She was 92 years of age at the time. Once after removing her false teeth as they were causing her pain, she placed them on the bench near some scraps for the birds. A few moments later she threw all the scraps for the birds off her back veranda, false teeth included. She was such a funny lady; she would always make you laugh and it was as if it was her responsibility to bring happiness and joy to all those around her.

Nan lived the last three months of her life at my parents' house. In this time, she had so much love, laughter and fun, it was such a special time – a gift from God.

Highlights of this time included going to the live theatre for the first time in her life to see *Singing in the Rain*. For weeks on end she would sing, 'I'm singing in the rain … I'm singing in the whatcha-ma-call-it'. This became a standard joke in the family and we ribbed her on every possible occasion.

At 93 years of aged Nan discovered the pop group 'Abba', and really enjoyed listening to the music. One day Mum and I put on a concert for her, singing various 'Abba' songs, Nan clapping excitedly with the music. We wore sparkling hats and costumes, we all laughed very much. 'You're both mad', she said laughing. During this time she discovered the beautiful song " *I have a dream*," particularly loving the verse 'I believe in angels'. Nan loved the lyrics so much that the song was repeated continually throughout the following weeks.

Nan had a deep faith, and would attend church as often as she could, but more importantly she lived her faith, in all the love and compassion that she gave to others.

As her health declined, we had no option other than to take her to hospital, as at the time it was difficult to obtain home oxygen. I was heartbroken as I wanted to nurse her at home until she died, but this was not to be.

Before leaving for the hospital, and quite confused because of transient ischaemic attacks, Nan whispered to me to 'stay by my side Trace, I am frightened'.

In hospital, her condition deteriorated within a few days and she was drifting in and out of consciousness. Our local minister came to pray for Nan and anoint her. We all joined hands around her bed as the minister prayed, and then suddenly Nan sat herself up and said 'I love the church', and then fell back into unconsciousness. Somehow, she had fought her way through the fog, and been able to muster up all the strength, to sit up and express this. We were all amazed. The minister claimed that he had never witnessed this before.

I have always believed that hearing was the last sense to go when one is dying, and have witnessed this hundreds of times over the years. This was once again demonstrated with Nan.

We kept a vigil around her bed for four days, but during this time she barely responded. When I was in her room with Nan, just the two of us, I whispered to her, 'You cannot do this while we are here can you?'. To my amazement there was a clear 'No'. I told her that we would leave and I would come back when she needed me, telling her how much I loved her and would miss her. Nan squeezed my hand and said, 'Love you darling'. At that time there was beautiful feeling of God's love and peace in the room. 'God is here', I said to her. 'And the angels?' 'Yes they are, the light is beautiful'. Once again she had fought through the fog of unconsciousness to speak to me for what would be the last time. I returned to the hospital and prepared Nan for her final journey – her favourite music playing in the background, her favourite blue nightie, and a little dash of pink lipstick as requested. Naturally at Nan's funeral we played *I had a dream*, and everyone left with a beautiful pink rose.

7

Charlie: An Angel By My Bedside

Charlie was 90 years old, living in an aged care facility. He was extremely angry with life, and in particular, God. Born into a strict Anglican family, of three brothers and one sister, Charlie was the eldest, and was expected to be the man of the house after his father suddenly died. There was much expectation on him, so not unnaturally he rebelled and eventually got himself into all kinds of trouble by mixing with the wrong crowds and subsequently making the wrong decisions. As he became older he became angrier; he lost his way, his faith and his hope, and his sense of self was gone; he was a lost soul.

Charlie married later in life and, according to him, this was the happiest period of his life, a time where this constant friend of 'anger' was no longer present, a time of peace and contentment, laughter and fun. Charlie had at last settled down. He spent 60 happy years with his wife, before his wife died and Charlie moved into an aged care facility. He then returned to his old ways, the angry old Charlie was back, the one which he had left behind many years ago. His anger was intensified with yet another problem – alcoholism. He drank a great deal both morning and night, and would become very aggressive towards the nursing staff, throwing whatever he could put his hands on. He was described as 'extremely difficult'. There had been several attempts to have Charlie evicted from the home because of his behaviour, but all had failed. However, I did not have difficulty in caring for Charlie as he had known my grandfather for many years and had great respect for him. This paved the way for me to try to connect with this 'difficult resident'. Little did I know when I had first meet Charlie with my grandfather many years previously, that I would be the one with him when he took his last breath.

Charlie had been diagnosed with aggressive bowel cancer which had metastasised to both his liver and his spine, and his health quickly deteriorated. As the palliative care nurse consultant, I was responsible for developing and implementing a palliative care end-of-life plan for Charlie. This was no easy task. Charlie's anger intensified, to the point that I was the only health care professional he would permit to enter the room without verbally abusing them. He denied God, his faith, heaven, and one could not approach anything of a spiritual nature with him. Once you were dead, you were dead; he just wanted to be left alone.

Charlie's journey by no means was easy; he continually took one step forward and three back; he was frightened, actually terrified as he later admitted to me, and it was this fear which prevented him from reaching out to others at a time when he needed it the most. Charlie was straight down the line, everything was black and white, there was no in between. One day as I entered his room, Charlie unexpectedly asked me if I knew a minister whom he could talk to. I was flabbergasted but thrilled. I suggested a local Anglican minister who was also a friend of mine. He looked at me with amazement and then said, 'I have a minister living in my home at the moment'. On asking the minister's name I was astonished to find out that it was actually my friend. Charlie had rented out his home when he had moved into the facility to live, as he did not want to sell the property. Charlie was dumbfounded. God was certainly working overtime. The chances of this occurring were even too remote for the biggest sceptic such as Charlie to deny.

Charlie was excited for the first time that I could recall. 'I must speak to him', he said with a real urgency in his voice. Within 24 hours a meeting was arranged between the two. After the encounter I went in to see Charlie. I could clearly see the change – the anger was gone, and was replaced with a serenity and peace. His face, which had been so tense, was now soft, his eyes gentle and sparkling, the snarl replaced with a genuine smile of warmth.

Charlie greeted me with a kiss on the cheek. He expressed that he had once again found God; he had reclaimed his faith, and was at peace.

That night Charlie stated that his room was full of brilliant white light and he clearly saw a most beautiful angel standing by his bed, just hovering over him. He believed that the angel was his beloved wife, just waiting for him to return home to God. For the next two nights the vision of the angel was present at the end of his bed, a magnificent beauty, projecting peace and love such as he had never before experienced.

Charlie had two more visits from the minister, and in that time he was able to ask for forgiveness for a variety of wrongs in his life for causing pain to others, for turning his back on his faith and his loving God. After the first visit from the minister, Charlie never drank alcohol again. I watched in amazement as he poured three bottles of whiskey down the sink.

I spent many days with Charlie just listening to his stories of his life, his regrets, his accomplishments and his great loves. He at last had established meaning to his life; he knew that God loved him, and had always been with him, actually 'carrying him', during the difficult times. There was no doubt in his mind that he would be reunited with his beautiful wife in heaven, and he was quite excited about the eventual reunion.

As I was leaving, he looked at me with tears in his eyes and asked if I would stay with him and hold his hand when he returned home to God, as he had no family. Naturally I agreed, and was extremely touched. This man had come full circle with his faith journey, never had I seen such a transformation of any soul, from such extreme anger, resentment, bitterness, to that of peace, acceptance and love. *'We delight in the beauty of the butterfly, but rarely admit the changes it has gone through to achieve that beauty.'* (Maya Angelou)

The next morning I arrived at work as I sensed in my heart that Charlie was waiting for me. Over the years of caring for the dying one gets to trust one's own intuition and is led by the Holy Spirit.

As I entered the room, Charlie gently whispered to me, 'I have been waiting for you my angel. Now I can go, all is in order'. He kissed my hand, clasping it to his chest, closing his eyes softly, and gently without effort took his last breath.

Angels

'When my time to die comes an angel will be there to comfort me. He will give me peace and joy even at that most critical hour, And usher me into the presence of God, And I will dwell with the Lord forever. Thank God for the ministry of his blessed Angels'.

Billy Graham

8

Helen: Your Hand in Mine

Sometimes during life, the Holy Spirit uses us as vessels to help others without our even being aware of it at the time. And the recipient of such actions may also be sent to help us in return – to be messengers of God.

One of these occasions occurred during my visit to the church Saint Augustine's by-the-Sea in Waikiki – Hawaii. The magnificent church is dedicated to Hawaii's first saint – Damien – who dedicated his life to caring for those with leprosy (Hansen's disease). Damien was born in 1840 and died at the age of 49, after having contracted the disease. Damien was canonised a saint on 11 October 2009. His canonisation was followed on 21 October 2012 by the canonisation of Sister Marianne Cope, for her work with Father Damien for over 30 years in nursing leprosy patients.

To attend Mass at this church, which is known in Hawaii for amazing spiritual phenomena and healing, was a blessing. The healing Mass was at 6 p.m. on Sunday evening. I decided to go 20 minutes early to ensure arriving on time.

It was Saint Therese's feast day (my patron saint) so it was especially special for me.

As I opened the large wooden doors to enter the church, I was surprised to see that it was already completely full – there was almost standing room only. Two white statues of angels were standing at each holy water font; they were approximately three feet tall, and appeared very life-like. I immediately became aware of a beautiful energy within the church.

There were brilliant stained glass windows that depicted certain characters from the Bible; the sun beamed on to each window reflecting radiant colours throughout the church. There was a large crucifix hanging high above the altar.

I managed to find a seat in a pew about 20 rows from the altar on the right side.

As Mass began the most beautiful Polynesian choir began to sing; the voices sounded so angelic and pure that it seemed as if the heavens were opening up and a choir of angels were descending to the earth. The gospel choir transported you far away as you listened to the words of praise and worship.

As I felt that I was in a crossroad in my life, I was quietly asking the Virgin Mary how she wanted me to serve – to continue to care for the dying? To change directions? – What was her plan for me? During this time of contemplation I felt as though I was nudged by heaven to open my eyes, slowly directing my head towards the left side of the church to glimpse a figure of a statue.

As I continued to gaze at the figure, I realised that it was indeed the Blessed Virgin Mary.

My eyes were firmly fixed. The more that I continued to gaze at the statue, the more she appeared to develop a life-like appearance, surrounded softly with a pure white light.

It was difficult to describe her beauty, she was illuminating with light – words were inadequate. I knew in my heart that I was witnessing an amazing blessing. I sincerely believe that she looked up at me and smiled. I kept watching her intently; the priest's words just drifted away, I could not take my eyes from her. Her left hand was reaching out to something or someone. 'What do you want of me?' I asked most humbly. Once again, her hand appeared to be gesturing toward something or someone. At the same time I was overcome with the most magnificent fragrance of roses, wafting gently all around me, yet there were none in the church. I looked around quietly to see if anyone else appeared to be experiencing the same phenomena.

I continued to observe the statue's hand; at this time I could clearly see another hand resting in the Virgin's and it was the hand of an old lady. During this time God's light was beaming through the beautiful stained glass windows onto the crucifix and Our Lady. The whole church appeared to reflect a magnificent vibrant light.

Quietly, I started to walk towards the altar to receive communion, once again asking the question, *What do you want of me?* In receiving Holy Communion I was directed to walk past the statue and saw that the hand that had been resting in the Virgin's hand was indeed that of an elderly lady. My question had been answered so clearly – that caring for the aged and the dying was not just my career but my vocation. When I returned to my seat there on the floor was a single rose petal, which had appeared from nowhere, on Saint Therese feast day. I was overcome and my heart deeply touched.

~

I will send down a shower of roses.

Saint Therese

~

After Mass, I felt compelled by the Holy Spirit to share my experience with the elderly lady. I discovered her name was Helen and she was 89 years of age. Looking deeply into her old eyes I could see that she was dying. Helen was sitting on a high cushion in a wheel chair, very close to the statue of the Virgin Mary. The level of her hand supporting her weary head was in exact alignment with the hand of the Blessed Mother. From where I was sitting Helen's hand was resting in that of the Virgin Mary's.

Helen was extremely thin and frail, and her colour was exceptionally poor. She was wearing a scarf around her head. She was so weak that it was an enormous effort to even raise her head to say hello. Helen had ovarian cancer which had metastasised throughout her body; her prognosis was extremely poor, with only a few weeks to live. She was currently in hospice care.

As I shared my story with Helen she embraced me, crying with pure joy. Her eyes, which had been lifeless and tired, once again sparkled with the light of God's love – her being radiated this bliss; her spirit was uplifted. There was a real soul connection between us, as soon as I told her I was a hospice nurse, she shared her most beautiful story with me.

Helen was aware that she would die very soon, she was physically and mentally exhausted and was ready to go home to heaven. She had a beautiful relationship with Our Lady and a very deep faith. Although she claimed that she was at peace with her imminent death, there was still one thing that concerned her. Helen wanted to make sure that she would not be alone spiritually when she died. To ensure this was not the case, she had been quietly been praying to the Virgin Mary with a special intention, 'Blessed Mother, please show me a sign that when I am ready to come home you will be there and place my hand in yours and escort me home to heaven.' My prayer has been answered, she said hugging me and placing her weak arms around me in a loving embrace. 'Now I am ready to go', she gently whispered to me as she kissed me on the cheek. Helen had now been given her sign, just as I had mine. Here two strangers were brought together by the grace of God to be messengers to one another, to bring love, hope, guidance and peace

The Serenity Prayer

God grant me
the serenity
to accept the things
I cannot change
courage to change
the things I can,
and the wisdom
to know the difference.

Reinhold Niebuhr

9

Betty: The Maid

Betty was 99 years of age, previously from Sydney, where she had lived for many years on the beautiful Darling Harbour. Yes, she was used to the good life, a beautiful home, which overlooked the Sydney Opera House, a yacht docked in the crystal blue harbour waters, and her selected entourage of hired help. This included her maid, Sophia, who had cared for Betty for over 30 years.

Diagnosed with advanced dementia and, later on, bowel cancer, Betty decided that it was best if she moved to Melbourne to live with her daughter and son-in-law. Unfortunately, this only lasted a few months before Betty was reluctantly placed into care. I nursed Betty for over 5 years and so grew to know her and all her mannerisms extremely well – we shared a special relationship. But no matter who came in to the visit, she would introduce me as the 'maid'. (I was in fact the unit manager).

One day when an official came from the government (Standard Monitoring team) to inspect the unit, Betty quickly met all those concerned at the door, welcoming them with open arms, and then promptly requesting the Maid, to please serve refreshments for our guests. Both the officials and I laughed quietly to ourselves as I began to prepare the morning tea. From that day on the title of 'Maid' was well and truly mine.

Eventually Betty's health declined dramatically; she was dying. Her confusion increased dramatically, to time, place and person. She became so disoriented and longed to go 'home'. As her condition deteriorated even further, however, amazingly the intense confusion made way to periods of extreme clarity. During these times Betty would have great insight into her own mortality. She wondered about God, heaven, angels, and who would be waiting for when she returned home to God. As she was Catholic she had a deep faith and a special relationship with the Virgin Mary. She stated that she had no fear and that death would be a 'welcome relief'; she was tired and ready to go. Her physical body had different ideas and it was several months later before Betty took her last breath.

The night before Betty died, as I entered her bedroom, instead of my normal greeting as the maid, she opened her arms and said, 'Here is my darling nurse'. I looked at her in amazement. 'I know that you are not my maid dear, you are an angel sent by God to be with me when I die. I have called you my maid all these years as I loved my Sophia and trusted her just as I do you, she looked after me too, and I miss her'. In that moment I realised that this beautiful old soul had referred to me as her maid, as it had given her comfort and security. I sat with Betty for two hours, listening to her stories of her younger days, her clarity was sharp, gone was the haze of dementia, which she had been lost in. Her insight and all that she shared was truly a blessing.

I sat with Betty until the small hours of the morning, holding her hand. In this time she quietly whispered, 'I see the most beautiful white light, and there is a woman all dressed in blue, she is beautiful, she is just holding out her hand, and asking me to come.' 'Go with her Betty that is the Virgin Mary, let go, it is okay, go on your journey.' Just as I finished the last words Betty surrendered into the light and into the Mother's arms.

~

Let nothing come between you and the light.

Henry David Thoreau

~

10

Gladys: Pink Flannelette Sheets

Gladys was 80 years of age, and was one of the first residents I cared for while working at an aged care facility until I was old enough to commence my nursing training. I was only 12 years of age. Gladys was of the 'old school' – very well groomed, beautifully spoken and a real lady. She also had a wonderful sense of humour and a deep faith.

Glad, as I called her, did however have one vice, and that was her daily outfits all had to be matching, and the colour of choice was always pink. This included pink underwear, skirt and blouse to match, pink jumper and even pink shoes. She also needed pink tissues, pink handbag and a little touch of pink lipstick.

When Glad retired to bed, it was the pink flannelette sheets and matching pillow cases which she adored, which gave her so much comfort and security, and made her feel like royalty. Of course, she wore her pink crochet bed jacket, and insisted on her pink underwear even for bed. The sheets had to be hand-washed every second day. She would like to change them; she used only her pink sheets for as long as I knew her. Luckily, she had four pairs so that we could interchange them. The staff had to be extra careful with them as the sheets were so old, that they were concerned about how many more washes they could withstand. After they were washed and dried, Gladys would sit in her room and remark on the freshness of them. There would then be the production of placing the sheets carefully onto her bed, ensuring that there were no wrinkles. Such a simple thing as flannelette sheets gave Glad so much pleasure and security. She was a pure delight, and a loving and beautiful soul.

Over the years Glad had fallen in love with old Albert, a 94-year-old resident, a dear man, quite lucid in his mental capacity but, alas, totally deaf. As I was so young, Glad would hand me notes of affection to pass onto Albert about having a rendezvous each day at 1 p.m. under the large oak tree. Of course, Glad had to bring out the pink parasol and the large pink trimmed hat for such a romantic meeting. She would wait patiently under the old tree for her true love to arrive in his wheelchair. They would sit together, occasionally holding hands, and if Albert was feeling brave a small kiss would be planted on Glad's cheek. In witnessing this, one was reminded of a scene from the film *Gone with the wind*, Glad looking ever the part of Scarlet O'Hara. And Albert, in his suit, with small bow tie, portrayed Rhett Butler beautifully, and even though he could not hear a word that Glad was saying, he politely smiled and replied, 'Yes dear.'

This romance went on for many years, until Albert sadly died. Glad was heartbroken, and so was her spirit. Something within her died that night along with Albert. Each day became a struggle; her grief was overwhelming.

One evening, as I assisted Glad into bed, she, having insisted that the pink flannel sheets be dried and put onto her bed and her best pink nighty to be worn with bed jacket to match, shared with me the mystery of the pink sheets. They had been her mother's, and each time that she needed to feel her gentle mother's presence she would lie on them; it was as if she could feel the warm embrace of her mother. She had kept them all those years.

My mind drifted to my own flannel sheets that my grandmother would have on my bed when I would go and stay with her. As I would climb into the snug bed, I felt so warm, safe, loved and secure within those sheets. I can still remember the fresh smell, as they would come in from the clothes line and be gently placed onto my bed, with so much love.

Glad continued to speak of her life, her loves and her challenges throughout her life. It was as if she was tying up all the loose ends, expressing what she needed to say, and letting the rest dissolve into the Ether. I believe healing occurred in that room that night, as issues that once worried her were no longer of concern; there was a real peace in the room. God's presence was so strong that even Glad commented on 'the beautiful feeling in the room, do you think it is angels?' Before going to sleep Glad kissed me, not goodnight, but goodbye. I could not help to think how beautiful she looked, all dressed in pink, quite angelic. That night, without any fuss, Glad drifted off to once again meet her beloved Albert under the old oak tree.

~

Blessed is the influence of one true, loving human soul on another.

George Eliot

~

11

Brother Joe: One Last Fish

Brother Joe, a 92-year-old man, was a member of the Catholic Franciscan community. He suffered from Alzheimer's disease, and was later diagnosed with advanced liver cancer. I had the privilege not only of nursing Joe, but also of being his friend for many years.

On first meeting, Joe gave me the nickname 'Sunshine', and this was the name which he called me up until his death. He and I would spend a lot of time discussing world events, religion, faith, prayer and the human spirit. In addition to his devotion to prayer, Joe enjoyed music of all kinds, and anything to do with the ocean, and in particular fishing.

Over the years, Joe had many adventures while he was living at the facility, and was always at the fore of any mischief. But the one adventure which remains in my mind is 'one last fish'. As Joe's health was deteriorating he decided to create a 'Bucket list'. One by one he ticked off his achievements, until there was only one last activity which he wanted to complete before he died, to go fishing one last time.

As a result of making this happen for Joe, a colleague and I took Joe and four other residents with severe dementia to the seaside for one week. This was to be a week of 'normalisation', away from the routine of nursing homes, where residents could enjoy activities of their choice, stay up late, go out for meals, have treats, such as fish and chips on the beach, paddle in the cold water and, of course, go fishing. This holiday turned out to be one of the most amazing blessings for all concerned. The pure joy in the residents' eyes, the

spark which was often diminished, was now replenished, the spirit
was alive. Everyone had the most wonderful time, and laughter filled
the air. In the evening, when transferring Joe into bed, he suddenly
developed a fit of the giggles, so much so that we all fell on to the bed
together, the laughter was contagious.

The next day, Joe rose early. Dressed in his warm windcheater,
tracksuit pants, and of course fishing hat, he sat quietly reciting his
morning prayers, I could not help but smile as he said, 'If I could just
catch one last fish, I would be ever so grateful – Amen.'

Joe sat in his wheelchair carefully positioned on the pier, for over
three hours, patiently waiting for what would be his last fish. As I
approached Joe I could not help but be deeply moved; his face was
beaming, eyes sparkling with pure delight, and a smile from ear to ear,
his spirit was truly alive. Fishing rod in one hand and rosary beads in
the other, he was ready.

Then it occurred – the much anticipated catch of the day. The
largest snapper that I have ever seen. Joe was so thrilled that he cried
with delight, his last wish was now complete. Next came the photo
of him proudly holding his prize fish for all to see. Other fisherman
approached Joe commending him on his catch; he looked extremely
proud as he held the fish firmly in his old hands, joy radiating
throughout his entire being. Suddenly, a glorious orange butterfly
fluttered gently onto Joe's shoulder, he was in a state of pure bliss.
For those few hours he was no longer Joe, the elderly man who was
slowly dying, he was Joe the mighty fisherman.

That evening we cooked the fish for dinner under Joe's instructions
and everyone enjoyed sampling the splendid catch of the day. That
night during his prayers I overheard Joe thank God for allowing him
'one last fish', before he returned home to heaven. This was a truly
beautiful vision to witness.

A few months later Joe's health deteriorated quickly, he was dying and he realised it.

It never ceases to amaze me the insight that the dying have into their own passing. He expressed that he was not frightened and looked upon dying as 'going home'. He had such a solid faith, having communion each day, spending countless hours in prayer and reading his Bible for as long as he was able. But more importantly, he tried to live his faith, by helping others in need. Showing kindness and compassion to those less fortunate.

I had a few days off work and during that period I had the strong sense that Joe was getting ready to go on his journey 'home'. When I returned to work I immediately went into Joe's room, to find him semiconscious, he had not been responding for some time. As I gently held his hand and spoke to him, he opened his eyes and said 'Sunshine, I have been waiting for you', giving me the most beautiful smile. He softly kissed my hand; clasping his precious rosary beads tightly to his chest while glancing lovingly at his crucifix he took his final breath.

All that was important to Joe was in that room, his rosary, Bible, and crucifix. Later, when I was washing Joe, I found, in his pyjama pocket over his heart, his photo of his beloved fish.

~

Watching a peaceful death of a human being reminds us of a falling star; one of a million lights in a vast sky that flares up for a brief moment only to disappear into the endless night forever.

Elisabeth Kübler-Ross

~

12

Audrey: The World Is a Stage

Audrey was 90 years of age, and was living with advanced dementia. She lived alone, and had refused to go into care. She had been an actress all her life, and was well known within the show business circuit. The world was a stage and according to Audrey, we were all the actors, with a part to play. Some were here only for a short performance, some for encores, and others for feature films. But regardless of performance, when the curtain eventually came down, and the performance was finished we all returned home to the one source – which was God.

Over the years Audrey had played many parts, from the loving wife, mother, friend and even mistress. She had starred in many musicals up until her late 70s. Even now she still had a beautiful, quite angelic, voice. Audrey enjoyed the showstoppers such as *Hey big spender*, and in particular *New York, New York*.

Her long-term memory was her salvation; she would reminisce about her life on the stage, the people she met, and the places that she visited. She would talk with such joy about 'Opening nights' – the excitement, the nerves and glamour, the beautiful dresses, the smell of cigars and the pop of champagne corks as the opening was deemed a success. Reporters, interviews and doting audiences were all part of this lovely lady's past.

Audrey lived a very glamorous life, but within that life there was also much tragedy. Loss of a daughter at a very young age due to breast cancer, and a few years later, the loss of her beloved husband. Through these dark times, it was her faith in God that she relied on to give her strength; she had an inner knowledge and comfort that one day all three would be reunited in heaven.

Even now, at 90 years of age, Audrey dressed the part of the beautiful actress; her blonde dyed hair was proudly worn in a short bob haircut, and her make-up and grooming were immaculate, including brightly coloured painted fingernails. She articulated with such distinction and authority that one would not dare ignore her instructions. However, her dementia, combined with a series of small strokes, eventually meant that Audrey had to reluctantly leave her home and go into care. As I was assisting this beautiful frail soul to pack up the last of her belongings, the sorrow and grief which she displayed was overwhelming. She had lived in the same home all her life for over 60 years, first as a young girl with her parents, and then with her own family. All her memories were contained within those walls, all the joys and sorrows, the rich tapestry of her life.

As I glanced back to her dining room, which was now so bare, the brightly coloured paintings on the walls were gone, the richly coloured rugs which made the room so cosy, no longer there, the furniture which she took so much pride in vanished, the only trace left in the room which showed that Audrey had even lived there was an Oscar Award which she had once won for 'Best actress'. It was now being used as a door stop. No one coming into that old home would ever know the amazing life of the wonderful woman who had lived there all those years, perhaps the Oscar may have given them a clue. Sometimes, I do not think that health care professionals understand the full extent of the sense of loss and grief that accompanies having to leave one's home and go into care.

As we shut the door for the last time, tears were streaming down her old cheeks, she turned to me and said, 'I am only going for my grandson you know, so that he realises that he did all he could for me.' Audrey stated very clearly that she would only be in the facility for 24 hours, would just stick around for dinner and to see what the entertainment was like. That night at the facility they just happened to be having a Hollywood musical evening. The residents were all dressed in their best evening attire, and Audrey choose to wear her red sequinned gown, and earrings which she wore for the opening of *New York, New York*. 'I cannot pass up one more night of music and Hollywood glamour. But after that, darling, it will be time to bring the curtain down … and return home to God.'

Even now in old age, Audrey played the part. She looked so beautiful. As she sat with the other residents, laughing and sipping on the champagne, sharing stories of her past life in the theatre, the other residents were in awe of her, waiting patiently with excitement to hear, 'You knew who?', 'What happened?', 'You're kidding, you did what?' Once again Audrey had an audience; she had charmed the whole room.

Within seconds, she was invited to join the band; her walking frame was quickly tossed to the side as she staggered up on the stage. She had a wonderful time; each song was theatrically belted out by Audrey to her adoring audience who encouraged her with loud singing, clapping and even a standing ovation. Audrey had returned to being the actress, singer and entertainer, the frail old lady with dementia was gone, her spirit was alive, and so was she.

Audrey had a fantastic time singing for all the residents and staff, all the famous show stoppers from *Chicago*, *God spell*, *My fair lady*, *42nd street*, *All that jazz*, and of course, *New York, New York*. To everyone's amazement the final song which Audrey chose to sing was Wish me luck as you wave me goodbye. This song would prove to be prophetic, by just the following morning.

That evening, after a wonderful time, Audrey insisted on wearing her sequined red gown and earrings to bed, she was ready for her biggest performance yet, and wanted to make a grand exit. As I was assisting her into bed she kept singing the words to *New York, New York*, 'Start spreading the news, I'm leaving today...', each word was sung with so much joy and clear anticipation. 'I am going home soon dear, I am very tired, I wish to thank you for all the love and care which you have given me over the years, you are a true friend.' As I sat holding her old hand, I could feel my eyes well up with tears; this was one goodbye which was going to be difficult. I sat with Audrey for over two hours – she had much she wanted to share with me. 'Do you think the angels will let me sing with them? Will God be happy to see me? Will he recognise me? Will my daughter and husband be waiting for me?' These were all questions that she pondered.

Audrey was extremely calm; she had no fear or anxiety, just a serenity and acceptance that she would soon be going to heaven, and be reunited with all those she loved. 'Dear, will you stay and hold my hand until God comes and replaces your hand with his?' – This was one of the most beautiful things that I had ever been asked to do. 'Of course I will', I whispered into her ear.

Although, the other health care professional in the facility felt that Audrey was being premature in her prediction, they respected her wishes for me to stay. I, however, knew only too well from experience to listen carefully to what Audrey was telling me, knowing that the aged often have a deep insight into their own passing and their own little glimpse of heaven.

I stayed with Audrey holding her hand until the small hours of the next morning. During this time Audrey spoke of the magnificence of the angels that she saw at the end of her bed throughout the night, the radiant white light which surrounded her, and the presence of God's love. I continued to hold her hand, softly singing to her 'Wish me luck as you wave me goodbye'.

Within a few gentle moments, and without effort, God gently replaced my hand with his, Audrey taking her final bow.

~

All the world's a stage and all the men and women merely players. They have their exits and entrances, and one man in his time plays many parts.

William Shakespeare (1813)

~

13

Bill: To My One Friend

Bill was 90 years of age with advanced dementia—Unfortunately , he was often neglected by those around him as communication was extremely difficult. Due to continual decline in cognition he could only articulate one or two words, which were usually disjointed .To many he was a "Silent" resident , but to others who could see beyond the disease progression and into the soul he had the most beautiful heart , and radiated pure Joy.

Bill could ambulate independently and would wander for hours around the unit, almost as if he was looking for someone or something; there was never any agitation or aggression, just a gentle peace about him, and always a smile.

Bill was an orphan; he had never 'belonged' to a family, to know what it was like to be loved, to have parents, brothers or sisters, let alone grandchildren, nor had he really ever had a true friend as he was shifted regularly from orphanage to orphanage throughout the country. This was his one great sadness in his life; he was lonely and needed love. Mother Teresa once said, 'The greatest disease is feeling unloved.' How true this is. The physical Bill may have gone, but his spirit was well and truly alive. He was exceptionally intuitive, and although he could not clearly express his intentions , his eyes reflected his beautiful spirit, there was a real spark in those eyes; they seemed to look deep into ones soul

~

The Eyes are the window to you soul.
William Shakespeare.(1564-1616)

Each birthday and Christmas would pass and no-one would come and visit Bill. The sadness on these occasions nearly broke my heart. The staff would try to compensate for Bill's not having any visitors. One Christmas, after much discussion with the management, I was given permission for Bill to come home with me for Christmas with my family. To be part of a family Christmas for the first time in his life – no better gift could have we have given him. The day was full of joy; he embraced everyone, giving hugs to both my parents, proudly shaking my brother's hand and playing with my young nephews. He was amazed at the colours of the brightly decorated Christmas tree, and insisted that the Christmas lights remain on for the whole day. He was overwhelmed; the spirit in this old man's eyes was once again ignited. He spoke more that day than I had ever heard him communicate in the years which I had nursed him, full sentences, no confusion with words- it was truly magical.

After few months Bill died peacefully. As the staff were cleaning out his drawers, they found a card addressed to me. When I opened the envelope I could clearly see that it had been made by Bill, and even though difficult to read and understand, one line read, 'To my one friend, love, your Bill.'

~

Be the living expression of God's kindness...
Kindness in your face,
Kindness in your eyes,
Kindness in your smile,
Kindness in your warm greeting.

Mother Teresa, (2003)

~

14

Chuckles: Keep Laughing

The concept of humour dates back to Plato and is even described in Proverbs in the Bible, 'A cheerful heart does good like medicine, but a broken spirit dries the bones'. (Proverbs 17.22) Florence Nightingale also considered laughter a good medicine: 'Painful expressions were better dismissed by a real laugh'. (Nightingale, 1860, p. 60) Evidence-based positive effects of humor include improving a resident's mood, and optimism, reducing anxiety, assisting with depression and overall coping with a terminal illness. (Dean, 1997; Tennant, 1995) Laughter also serves as an outlet for anger, provides a healthy escape from reality, and lightens all the heaviness associated with illness, death and dying. When appropriate, humor and laughter are powerful ways of caring for the spirit in end of life.

For the purpose of this story this resident will be called by his clown name, 'Chuckles'. Chuckles was 90 years of age, he had advanced dementia with various other medical complications. Some days his confusion and disorientation was worse than others. Lucid moments were becoming less frequent. His short-term memory was extremely poor, yet as with most residents with dementia, his long-term memory was his salvation. He had lived at the facility for over 10 years so he was well known and loved by all the nursing staff, and other residents. Chuckles grew up in the circus, it was in his blood. Both of his parents were performers so naturally when he was old enough he too joined the travelling circus.

When our paths first crossed Chuckles gave me the nickname 'Sparky'. This name has stuck with me ever since, and was the name which I registered when I to became a professional clown over 20 years ago.

Chuckles spent his life bringing laughter and joy to people of all ages, especially young children. During these years he met his wife who was a fellow performer – a clown named 'Bubbles'. They were married for over 40 years, but alas could not have children. Therefore the children who Chuckles and Bubbles performed for became their family – they had children all over the world. The big top and all that went with it were a part of their lives that brought so much joy. This included the anticipation and excitement of opening night as the main tent was erected, preparation of the trapeze and high wire, safety nets, and the transportation of the animals which were beautifully cared for and loved. There was also the smell of fresh sawdust as it was placed in the ringmaster's circle, the ironing of beautiful costumes, sequined outfits, feathers, leotards, diamantes, and the perfume of make-up and hairspray. Others were the smell of fresh fairy floss as it oozed out of the machines, toffee apples, gas balloons, and carnival activities, as they were prepared for the oncoming crowds.

These were only a memory for Chuckles now; all that remained was a tattered shoe box that contained his treasures from his life in the circus. A red nose, a well-worn clown horn, an entry ticket to the bigtop, several old photos of him and his wife as clowns, a yellow plastic daisy, a water pistol, a brightly coloured magic scarf and a small sequined bow tie, that used to flash on and off. There was also another shoe box, which he never let anyone open. However, it would not be long until this mystery was shared. To Chuckles, making people laugh and smile was an important part of his daily routine. He would go out of his way to make the other residents, staff and visitors laugh. He had a wonderful sense of humour and mischief. Even though his dementia was advanced he still managed to tap into his inner spirit and create laughter wherever he went. 'Keep laughing' was his motto.

Chuckles also had a deep faith in God, and would attend church on a regular basis. Before each clown performance, he and his wife used to ask God to please be with them and let them be a vessel for laughter, to make others happy, to let them escape their troubles, if only for a short time. It was his faith in God that he relied upon to get him through difficult times. There was no doubt in his mind that when his time on earth was finished he would return home to his heavenly father and be reunited with his 'Bubbles'.

How Chuckles longed to go to the circus just once more before he died, to know that his life had purpose and meaning. As only God could have organised it, a circus was coming to town. I arranged to take Chuckles and two of his closest friends to a performance for his 90 birthday. Unknown to Chuckles, I visited the circus the day before and spoke to the ringmaster to arrange a private tour of the circus after the performances, also mentioning that it was Chuckle's 90th birthday. Not only was a tour arranged as a special surprise, but the ringmaster stated that he had also known Chuckles' parents.

The day came for the big adventure. The three friends were dressed in their best attire waiting patiently in the foyer for me to arrive. Chuckles wore his favourite blue shirt, with bow tie to match, very dapper, but as I glanced down, the three broke into contagious laughter as Chuckles had on his brightly multicoloured clown pants. Yes, he had taken them out of storage, dusted them off and was wearing them with much pride. This was the mystery of the other shoe box.

When we arrived at the big top we were ushered to our seats as if we were VIPs; ringside seats had been arranged. No visit to the circus would be complete without fairy floss. As the beautifully dressed woman in an exquisite blue sequined gown surrounded with elegant feathers approached, Chuckles called out, 'Four please Miss Feathers'. He then took his old wallet out of his pocket, and his frail old hand carefully selected the correct amount of money for the mouth-watering floss.

Then it commenced, the band started, lights flashed magnificent colours around the tent's arena, the ringmaster, tall, dressed in a black tails, sequined red cummerbund and top hat, walked proudly into the ring. As I glanced at Chuckles, his eyes were sparkling with joy, his spirit was alive, he was home, where he belonged. For a few short hours he would be 'Chuckles' the clown, back in his familiar territory. As the acts began his spirit became even more alive, smiling and clapping at every opportunity. The clowns came on, 'Be a clown, Be a clown.' Looking at Chuckles I could see him singing all the words, without any confusion, and with so much pride.

The clowns in brightly coloured costumes, made everyone laugh and scream with excitement as they attempted magic tricks, while the performing dogs chased the clowns endlessly around the ring, and of course the performance was finalised with a pie-throwing contest. The laughter was contagious. The three old men sitting next to me were no longer old; their spirits had resorted back to being young, all confusion was gone, fragility was no longer important, nor was being defined by a disease or as an aged person – all that was important was the spirit, the spirit of laughter, of joy, and of freedom of expression.

As I sat just watching the joy on their faces the most wonderful event occurred. The youngest of the clowns came over to Chuckles with the microphone and said, 'Today ladies, gentleman, children, we have a very special friend in the audience. This man was my inspiration in becoming a clown, I would go to see him every weekend when I was growing up, and he brought so much happiness into my life that I too wanted to become a clown. Ladies and gentleman please join with us to wish our friend Chuckles a happy birthday.'

Chuckles was overcome with emotion; tears of joy filtered down his face like a stream and the spark in his eyes reflected sheer joy.

Two more clowns escorted him into the arena. The spotlight was once again on this beautiful old soul, he was back where he belonged; his frail body did not stop him from getting into the clown car with assistance from the other clowns. It was a magical moment for all concerned. The ringmaster then returned with a birthday cake in the shape of a clown face. All the other performers then joined the audience in singing *Happy birthday*. Chuckles was in his element, with the meaning of his life being validated by all. To know that he had inspired the young clown into spreading laughter around the world was all that Chuckles needed to know; everything was in order.

A few months later, Chuckles' health declined rapidly. He spoke openly about dying; it was time, he was tired. There was no fear, just peace. He wondered who he might see in heaven, even pondering if God had a good sense of humour. To this he would say, 'He would have to have as he made humans.' He prayed daily, and spent time with his local Minister. Up until a day before he died, Chuckles still reminisced about his day at the circus, going through every detail, with such happiness. Chuckles died peacefully in his sleep, without effort and with a gentle smile on his face.

As I was packing up his belongings I found a brown paper bag, carefully tied with a pink ribbon. This was addressed to 'Sparky the Clown'. When I opened the parcel it contained a red clown nose, a very old piece of butchers' paper, which had the clowns prayer written on it in pencil, at the bottom of the page there was a personal message:

~

"Keep laughing and smiling Sparky. Love, your friend Chuckles".

~

The clown's prayer

As I stumble through this life, help me to create more
laughter than tears,

Dispense more happiness than gloom,

Spread more cheer than despair.

Never let me become so indifferent that I will fail to see
the wonder

In the eyes of a child, or the twinkle in the eyes of the
aged.

Never let me forget that my total effort is to cheer people,
make them happy

And forget at least momentarily

All the unpleasantness in their lives.

And, in my final moment, may I hear you whisper:

When you made my people smile, you made me smile

Author Unknown

15

Youshi: The Catholic

I only had the honor of nursing Youshi for one night, and it was the night that he died. His final journey home to God was one of grace, wonder, love, and tremendous trust.

He was only fifty years old, originally from Japan, and had lived in Australia for ten years, since he married. In that time he and his wife had a son, who was 6 years of age. Youshi married an Australian woman called Alice, which went against his parents' wishes, as they were extremely traditional in their beliefs and this also included their religion. He was so frail, and thin, but had a beautiful smile, that even when so ill would melt the hardest of hearts. His parents had come from Japan and were overseeing his care.

As the night progressed Youshi and I were alone for a period of time, and he called me over to his bedside. He had noticed the cross which I wore around my neck, commenting on it. He then shared with me that unbeknown to his parents, he had converted to Catholicism, like his wife. He was so thrilled as he shared his story with me. Friends had also been instrumental in this occurring. He had such a deep devotion to Jesus and Our Lady, showing me the brown scapular which he wore around his neck, but out of sight from his parents. As he continued to speak he said, " I prayed that before I die, someone would come, who I could talk to freely about my love of the Virgin Mary, and here you are". I was both touched and extremely humble.

I discussed with Youshi about the possibility of sharing his story with his parents before he died and to tell them that he had become Catholic. At first he was reluctant, and was frightened of rejection, but as the night wore on he began to contemplate this. I sat by his bed and at his request read him passages from the Holy Bible. Gently in the background some hymns were playing, *"Come as you are, that's how I want you…"*. I commented on the hymn and the beautiful words. With this Youshi said, "Yes, come as you are, that's all I need to do".

As he said this there was the most beautiful feeling of serenity and peace within the room. A few minutes later his parents returned, and quietly and confidently with all the support from Heaven he told his parents that he had converted to Catholicism and had never been happier.

To Youshi's surprise, his parents cried and said, "If that is where you have found God then that is wonderful". I left the family for over 20 minutes for special time together, a time where healing occurred I am sure, and great love was expressed.

Later on that night a Catholic Priest had been called to come and give Youshi the Holy Communion and the Last Rites. He was surrounded by his family when he died, with his Bible in his hands… he died a Catholic.

~

We seek for the meaning of our lives,
inevitably by illness, suffering and death
often through our spiritual dimension.

Pierre Teilhard de Chardin

~

16

Millie: The Party

For over 6 years I was unit manager at a specialised 10 bed Dementia Unit. I made it my responsibility to ensure that the facility was made to feel as homely as possible for the residents, where normalisation was part of daily activities. Each resident was diagnosed with some form of Dementia, whether it was due to the normal aging process or Alzheimer's disease. As I worked there full time I knew each resident and their families exceptionally well. Each individual had their own unique story to tell and a character of their own, but all formed a family like atmosphere and cared for one another deeply.

Millie was a beautiful old soul a little lady, with pure white hair and piercing blue eyes, always smiling and on for a chat and cuddle. Not only did Millie have Dementia, but she also had advanced Cancer, which had metastasised throughout her body. She was becoming extremely tired and weak, but somehow still radiated sunshine to all that crossed her path.

Millie also possessed a very deep faith, in God, Jesus & Heaven. She would always pray every night and would often speak of seeing angels in her bedroom. The angels were her friends and gave her tremendous comfort.

Millie's 95 Birthday was approaching. She was so excited, her old eyes radiating light from her pure Joy as she spoke of her friends visiting from interstate to help celebrate this milestone. Each day she would inquire with such delight how many more days until her friends would arrive. She did not have a family as she was brought up in an orphanage – where she was very unhappy.

On the special day I arrived at work early afternoon in order to assist Millie with her chosen outfit for the evenings outing. Hair, nails and makeup were all complete; she looked so beautiful and was waiting patiently for her friends to come. Then it occurred, the unexpected phone call, due to unforeseen circumstances Millie's friends had to postpone the visit. My heart sank, as I placed the phone down, and gently broke the news to Millie. The light in her eyes, diminished immediately, the spark vanished her old face displayed such sadness as she gently cradled her head in her old hands and cried softly.

As I looked around the room I noticed that the mood within the facility was extremely quiet and the ladies all looked down and sad for their friend. As God would have it, I was to work a double shift so it was time for action. I called a colleague of mine and explained what had occurred. In return he went Party shopping, buying sausage rolls, party pies, pizza, chips, lollies, balloons, ice-cream, lemonade and the most beautiful Chocolate Birthday Cake.

That night in-between assisting the residents into their night attire, I managed with the assistance of my colleague to decorate the day room with streamers, Pink balloons, and a large Happy Birthday sign. One by one the ladies returned to the day room, all thrilled to see what had transpired. Naturally, last to come was Millie. She entered the room, as all her friends yelled "Surprise". It was one of the most beautiful occasions that I have ever witnessed. Millie's, eyes filled up with tears, as she clapped her hands with excitement, her old eyes once again filled with Joy the spark had been reignited. The other residents all gathered around her to wish her a Happy Birthday. As I stood watching I remembered a quote "A family is where two or more people gather." Yes, this was a family, all these residents were connected on such a spiritual level.

Sitting around the table the ladies started to chat to one another, laughter was contagious, hands were being held, and smiles exchanged.

When the delicious party food appeared, faces lit up with excitement the smell of hot pizza, pies, and sausage rolls wafted throughout the room. These were quickly eaten. Followed by chips, lollies, and ice-cream. And what would a party be without a Birthday Cake. After singing Happy Birthday to Millie, the residents all enjoyed a sing-along around the piano for over one hour.

Tired, full and happy all the residents were assisted to bed. My colleague and I cleaned up the mess, throwing away all the old food, to this day no one ever knew what transpired that night. As I removed the pink balloons I thought that I would take them around to Millie for her bedroom, to remind her of the wonderful night which she and the other residents had shared. As I approached her room, I was taken back to see this beautiful old lady, kneeling by the side of her bed, with the nights light from the moon outside her bedroom window shinning brilliant light onto her entire being saying her prayers.

"Thank you God, for my family here, and Thank you for my first ever party, I am ready to come home now, whenever you want to come for me." I stood quietly by the door, I could feel a tears rolling gently down my cheeks. Millie had never had a party before in her whole life. Entering the room I assisted her back into bed. Millie kissed me on the cheek. "Thank you my darling, that was the most wonderful party God Bless you always".

The next day I came to work to find out that Millie had died peacefully in her sleep on her Birthday, after having the most wonderful send off.

~

As I live each day, may I do my part,
To make a difference, to touch one heart.
And through each day, may it be my goal,
To encourage one mind, and inspire one soul.

Author Unknown

~

17

Lawrence: Are there Horses in Heaven?

Lawrence was 94 years of age, living in a residential care facility. As a younger man he had worked as a jockey for many years; he loved the horses and the excitement of the race track.

Laurence lived with dementia and various other medical conditions, but it was the usual progression of old age which saw his physical condition deteriorate.

Lawrence spoke of dying a great deal, but there was no fear; he was fascinated about the possibility of being reunited with all those who had gone before him. He had a deep faith and practised this on a daily basis while receiving comfort from attending the weekly Church service in the facility. Lawrence would spend countless hours sharing the stories of his adventures at the stables, the brushing down of the horses' coats so that they were shining, polishing saddles and bridles so that they would sparkle in the sunshine as the horse proudly raced past the punters – this was his passion in life.

Melbourne Cup Day quickly approached – this was one of Lawrence's favourite times of year. The nurses decided to create their own Cup Day celebrations for the residents to enjoy. The day room was all decked out with brightly coloured tables, roses as centre pieces, and crystal champagne glasses with chilled champagne. A variety of coloured balloons were strung up, and the carpet was scattered with fresh hay. Anything to do with horses, racing or the Cup was used to create the atmosphere. Large umbrellas on each table, while bridles, horse blankets and saddles were carefully placed around the room. A large wooden horse was made by one of the creative staff members, and this would play a role in the day's activities.

The ladies were all dressed in their best dresses; large brimmed hats, ribbons and bows were displayed with pride, while the men looked so handsome in suits, bow ties and even top hats. Lawrence was dressed in his old racing jacket and cap, with the brightly coloured sash which he had won at the Melbourne Cup when he was a jockey proudly displayed across his old chest. His face reflected such joy, with his eyes sparkling as the passers-by stopped to inspect his sash; his spirit was alive, he had rekindled his own meaning and purpose in life.

For the sweep Lawrence was in charge of calling out the names of the horses and jockeys. He was overwhelmed with emotion when in actual fact his horse came in first place; he had no idea how that eventuated, and put it down to God giving him one last 'flutter', before he died.

That night, after a wonderful day full of laughter, reminiscences and great fun, while I assisted Lawrence into bed, he gave me a hug and with tears in his eyes, expressing that he had the most 'joyous day' and he was now ready to go. But before closing his eyes for the last time he quietly inquired, "Do you think there are horses in heaven?"

~

"People are like stained – glass windows. They sparkle and shine when the sun is out, but when the darkness sets in, their true beauty is revealed only if there is a light from within."

Elisabeth Kübler-Ross

~

18

George and Father Bernie: Have You Seen My Teeth?

Father Bernie was the Catholic priest at the aged care facility where I was working. Although he was approaching 90 years of age, he still delivered daily Mass for the residents and gave pastoral care to those who were dying. He was loved by many, had a great sense of humour, and was extremely devoted to caring for the other residents.

George was dying from advanced metastatic cancer. He and Father Bernie had been close friends for many years. They were always playing practical jokes on one another, and we all waited in anticipation to see what the other one planned to catch their friend out.

George requested Holy Communion to be brought to his room each day. He spent many hours preparing for his imminent death. He was not frightened, as he had a deep faith, which had sustained him all his life. His life had been full of adventure and meaning. His life had been service to the sick and poor; he spent many years as a missionary in remote parts of Africa. He had also been a dentist, and had many wonderful stories of the children who he had assisted over the years. There was no doubt in his mind that God had called him to work as a missionary in Africa.

As George's condition deteriorated, the only thing which he seemed to be anxious about was that when he died that he departs this world with his false teeth in his mouth. This was very important to George. It became a standard joke between George, Father Bernie and the nursing staff. George was reassured that this would occur.

George told his friend that once he was in heaven he would send him a sign, to let him know that he was alright. To this Father Bernie just laughed, but could not help but wonder what his friend would arrange.

Just before George died, his teeth were cleaned once more and placed into his mouth. A few minutes after this, he took his last breath, peacefully and without effort, surrounded by his family and of course his dear friend Father Bernie.

Naturally Father Bernie was to conduct the funeral, but because of his age and the fact that he was extremely frail, it was decided that he would be accompanied by one of the younger priests. The day was raining, the ground extremely wet and slippery. After the beautiful church service, the procession went to the cemetery for the final committal ceremony. As Father Bernie leaned forward for the committal, the ground under him disintegrated, the mud making him slip. As a reflex action the young priest with Father Bernie grabbed onto Father Bernie's tassel on his robes. This prevented him from falling into the plot. But as this occurred, Father Bernie was jerked so hard, that his loose fitting false teeth fell out of his mouth and directly onto the casket. All everyone could do was to laugh, and to Father Bernie this was his parting gift from his friend of many years, who was now resting in the palm of God's hands.

~

He laughs best who laughs last.
                                        Sir John Vanbrugh

~

19

Arthur the Accident-Prone

The day had come; my new colleagues and I were escorting several of the residents on a bus trip to the Channel Nine studios in Richmond to see the taping of a local television game show. It was only my second week at this particular aged care facility, therefore I did not really know the residents, or other staff members very well, but I volunteered as the registered nurse to accompany everyone on the adventure. For some strange reason no other nurse put up her hand for the excursion and I was to find out by the end of the trip why this was so.

All the residents were enjoying a sing-along as the bus made its way toward the Richmond studios. As we approached the main gates, the bus driver went over a large speed hump. Even though the driver was going very slowly, and the residents all had safety belts firmly across their chests, and were safe and secure, one of the elderly men, who was extremely tall, rose in his seat, high enough to hit his head on the bus roof. There was blood everywhere. I rushed up and applied pressure to his head with a bandage. The bus driver was distressed, as were the other residents.

As we pulled up to the kerb, I saw near the TV studio a sign saying medical surgery now open. Naturally I escorted the old man into the surgery. This was where the fun began. Firstly, the doctor did not have a nurse on duty and needed some help to put two small stitches into Arthur's head, so I needed to gown up and assist. At the same time as this was occurring, a funeral director came in, to collect a deceased patient. Seeing this, the bus driver thought to himself, 'Oh my goodness I have killed him'. He was beside himself.

Eventually I came out with Arthur, to find the bus driver white-faced, sitting on a chair crying, clasping his head in despair and praying to God. When he eventually saw us he was overwhelmed with gratitude. Arthur's head was bandaged like a mummy in a movie, and all that could be seen was his large Italian nose.

As we got back onto the bus to go home, Arthur would not hear of it; he had waited all his life to go into a TV studio and was not going to leave now when he was so close. 'I don't even have a headache', he stated. After much discussion with both Arthur, the doctor and my other colleagues, we continued on to the studio. Although Arthur was stable with no signs of concussion, I still felt concerned.

As we entered the studios, all the residents were ushered to their seats. The lights in the studio were very strong, and there were cameras everywhere. Arthur was so excited, as were all the other residents.

Then the taping commenced. 'Quiet in the studio please.'

As I glanced at Arthur to ensure that he was alright, all that I could see was his large nose protruding from beneath the bandages. He looked like an Egyptian Mummy with the bandages all around his head. I could not help but get the giggles, and before long, the whole studio was in hysterical laughter. So much so, that the producer of the show called 'Cut', and came up to see what all the commotion was about.

The next thing we knew Arthur was requested to come down onto the television set, and naturally I had to assist him. He was given many special prizes for coming when he was injured, and even had a photo taken with the host of the show. He was thrilled. His eyes sparkled with joy, as he stood proudly displaying his battle wounds, all bandaged. What commenced as a disastrous day, turned out to be a wonderful day, with so much laughter.

When we returned to the facility, the staff all laughed, as apparently wherever Arthur went chaos followed, this being the reason why the other nurses never want to go on outings when Arthur is attending.

But for Arthur himself, he had a wonderful day and proudly displayed his photo next to his bed for all to admire.

~

A day without laughter is a day wasted.

Charlie Chaplin (1889)

~

20

George: My Old Friend

I first meet George when I was completing my nursing training at a Melbourne-based hospital. He had suffered a right-sided stroke, which had left weakness down the left side of his body. The stroke had also affected his speech and he had aphasia, finding it extremely difficult to articulate what he was trying to say. If given time, he could get words out, but whole sentences, particularly in the beginning, were extremely challenging. George had a long road ahead of him, if he was to function adequately once again.

George was a beautiful old man, with piercing blue eyes, receding hair, and a gentle and kind face. I nursed him for many months, and eventually, with the aid of a walking stick, he was able to ambulate with full supervision.

He had a very supportive and loving family who would visit him at least three times a week. George would so look forward to the visits, particularly from his daughter, whom he was extremely close to. The day when my rotation on that ward finished was one of mixed emotion for me, as I had really loved that particular ward and the wonderful patients that I had been privileged to have nursed. I left George until last to go and say goodbye to, as I knew that this would be difficult. As I approached his bed, he looked at me with tears in his eyes and gestured for me to look in his locker. When I opened the drawer there was a beautifully wrapped small box, and a card with my name on it. I was overcome. As I opened the box, I saw a silver nurse's fob watch from George and his family. I could not help but cry. The card was handwritten by George, and although certain words could not be understood due to his stroke, the words which I could read were, *Thank you Trace, Love George.* He had told the manager of the hospital what he was doing and it was all approved, as usually nurses are not permitted to accept gifts from patients or their relatives. But luckily for me they made an exception. I continued to use this fob watch in the future years of my nursing career.

George's family eventually asked me to come and private nurse George at their home, a few days a week. This occurred for over two years. In that time, I travelled with the family on holidays to Queensland were we had much fun and laughter. I remember George saving up all his one dollar coins for the pokie machines, not that he was a gambler, but we were at Queensland's finest casino. I watched him as he patiently placed the coins into the slot, the bells ringing when he won $100 – he was overjoyed. His whole face lit up with pure happiness.

George also enjoyed a glass or two of Jack Daniels, which he would insist on before dinner. He had a great sense of humour and was always laughing or winking at me when he tried to tell a joke. Once, when assisting him into bed, George laughed so hard that his daughter, George and I collapsed on the bed together in fits of laughter.

George also had a holiday house down at the beach, so I would often accompany the family down to the home as his private nurse. This too was a fantastic time, full of very happy memories and great fun. George continued his life with the full assistance of his devoted family and friends, until he was eventually diagnosed with bowel cancer which had metastasised to various other organs. He still kept the fighting spirit which I knew him for, until eventually he had to go into care as his family could no longer lift him. This broke their hearts. Never have I witnessed such a devoted family.

I was not with George when he died, and I did not have the chance to say goodbye. But the day that he died, my fob watch stopped. I felt that was his way of saying goodbye. He knew that I loved him, and one day when my time on earth is up, I hope that he is waiting in heaven with the Jack Daniels on ice.

~

There are souls in this world which have the gift of finding joy, everywhere and of leaving it behind them when they go.

Fredrick Faber

~

21

Philomena: The Bubble Bath

Philomena was a treasure, a wonderful lady with a great sense of humour. Over the four years that I nursed Phil, I got to know her extremely well and also her lovely family. Phil had dementia, so had been placed into residential care, but her family were extremely devoted to her, especially her daughter.

One morning I decided to give Phil a bubble bath, for relaxation. I went into the bathroom to fill the large spa bath, adding a cap of bubble bath. I then returned to Phil's bedroom to help her gather her toiletries and clothes for the day. I asked a colleague to check the bath, while I was assisting Phil with her choices. Unbeknown to me, my colleague saw the bubble bath, and thinking that I had not put any liquid into the bath, poured another two capfuls into the water.

When Phil and I entered the bathroom, the bubbles had barely started to build, and I thought in my great wisdom, that this was no bubble bath, hardly any bubbles, so I added another capful of liquid. I then assisted Phil into the bath and helped her with her wash. This was interrupted by a knock at the door, and a staff member wanted to ask me a question. Staying in the room next to Phil, and turning my back for seconds to answer the question, all I could hear was this out of control giggling, and laughter at the top of her voice. I turned to Phil to see the bath over flowing with bubbles and her little grey head popping out from the top, beneath all the fluffy white foam. She was hysterical with laughter having a wonderful time. She said she felt like she was an angel floating up in the clouds. My colleague and I stood there also laughing at this beautiful old soul's joy with something so simple. The joy was contagious, before long we were all in fits of laughter.

Phil then said, 'Come here, I want to show you something.' I came close and with one huge sweep of bubbles I was covered from head to toe. They were everywhere, overflowing from the bath, all over Phil, and completely over me! She was completely satisfied with her victory; I was soaked. This was war. Bubbles started being thrown far and wide, it was one of the funniest visions I have ever witnessed. This little 90-year-old lady scooping up handfuls of foam, and throwing it joyfully into the air, at me, and even my colleague got soaked.

After a good 30 minutes, I assisted Phil out of the bath, which then took a further 20 minutes to drain from all the foam. Her old eyes sparkled with the joy she had experienced, her spirit was alive.

A few months later, Phil's condition deteriorated and she was dying. Although she was drifting in and out of consciousness she knew that both her daughter and I were sitting with her.

I eventually had to leave Phil as it was my Nan's birthday and we were having tea together. During dinner Nan suddenly said, 'Now you need to go, you are needed'. I had not said anything to Nan about Phil, yet Nan knew – I think that she had a nudge from God. This Nan was so tuned into the Holy Spirit, that this was most likely the case.

When I returned to the facility Phil's daughter was both shocked and happy to see me as she was coping by herself with her mother's impending death. I remember looking out into the nights sky as we continued to sit with this beautiful old lady, the moon was glorious, reflecting radiant light which beamed through the curtain and onto Phil's, face. As the light reflected onto her entire being, she gave a gentle smile. Had this been the light of God which she had seen?

I continued to sit with them both until the small hours of the morning, and just as the sun gently rose to declare a new day this beautiful old soul let go of her physical body, and her spirit transcended into the heavenly realms.

~

Shoot for the moon. Even if you miss, you'll land among the stars.

Les Brown

~

22

Kalighat - Mother Teresa's Home for the Dying and Destitute - Calcutta- India

Perhaps one of the most profound experiences in my life as a nurse was the time I spent at Kalighat, Mother Teresa's home for the Dying and Destitute in Calcutta – India.

Mother Teresa was born on 26 August 1910. She was originally given the name Agnes Gonxha Bojaxhiu. A Catholic nun from Albania, she worked in Calcutta. While travelling from Calcutta to the convent in Loreto in Darjeeling for annual leave in September 1946, she experienced what she called 'the call within the call'. She was to leave the convent and help the poor of Calcutta, while living amongst them. To Mother Teresa this was an order, and to fail would have been to break the faith.

The Sisters of Charity were founded in Calcutta, India by Mother Teresa in 1950, and she spent the next 45 years as a humanitarian and advocate for the poor, ministering and caring for the sick, dying and destitute.

Mother Teresa died on 5 September 1997; following her death was beatified by Pope John Paul and given the much deserved title of 'Blessed Mother Teresa of Calcutta'. In 2016 Mother Teresa was declared a Saint by Pope Francis at the Vatican in Rome and given the name Saint Teresa of Calcutta.

Here I was in Calcutta about to enter the large gates for the first time to Kalighat. I was overwhelmed by the unconditional love and compassion that the young Sisters of Charity gave to those in their care. Working quietly and with joy among the poorest of the poor, with diseases such as cholera, typhoid, leprosy and HIV, nothing made a difference to the Sisters. In each person they nursed they saw the body of Christ. Both the physical and spirit was cared for, this was holistic care.

Here I witnessed faiths of all descriptions, Christianity, Hindu, Muslim – it did not matter. Nor did the colour of one's skin, or the language that one spoke. Both the Sisters and those who worked and died at Kalighat were bound by an invisible band of humanity. People would lie on the floor on an old mattress with a blanket and pillow, if they were lucky. Meals were usually rice. Everything was used at Kalighat. Nothing was thrown out as rubbish, everything had a purpose.

There was a sign outside the entrance of the home which read 'God's work has to be done in his own way, and he has his own means of making our work known'. I have always remembered those words. I felt so at home at Mother Teresa's and consider it one of the most humbling and amazing experiences of my life.

Two years later I returned to Kalighat and there was this tremendous feeling of 'coming home', as I entered the large gates once again. I remember witnessing a young Sister of Charity, probably no older 20 years of age, cradling a woman with leprosy in her arms as she was dying. The woman was speaking to the Sister in her native tongue, 'I have lived like an animal on the streets and now I will die like an angel – I surrender.' She then closed her eyes and died peacefully and without effort. Witnessing this had a huge impact on me both emotionally and spiritually. This woman, like many others, received three of the most important gifts that I believe may be given to another human being – that is, to feel wanted, loved and touched.

Calcutta was in my heart and soul – the people I met, the Sisters' compassion towards the dying and Mother Teresa's endless, joy and love in caring for the dying and serving God. She had so much trust and tremendous faith; if God wanted something to happen, it would, and otherwise it was not important. It was this faith, combined with the unconditional love which both Mother Teresa and the Sisters of Charity demonstrated to strangers, to those who they would gather from the streets of Calcutta that made Kalighat such a beautiful spiritual haven. From early morning to late at night the Sisters would attend to each person, ensuring that pain was under control; each individual would be bathed or sponged and cleaned, and many people too weak to walk would be carried by volunteers, in order to have a bath. I observed one young man gently lifting an elderly man into his arms and carrying him to the wash room. The old man, although obviously dying, still managed to smile and wave gently to me as he approached me. As I reached out to touch his hand, his eyes lit up, the spark was still there, and the spirit was still alive. Although everyone at Kalighat was dying, there still was this amazing sense of 'spirit' reflected in people's eyes. A gentle touch could bring so much comfort and joy. At times diseases were so bad – leprosy which was still rife would result in gangrene, wounds so necrotic that the odour would be overwhelming – yet the Sisters did not flinch but smiled lovingly as they attended to the care. It was then that I realised that the Sisters were not looking at the broken bodies, the poverty, or disease, but that of the human spirit.

~

There is a light in this world, a healing spirit more powerful than any darkness we may encounter. We sometimes lose sight of this force when there is suffering, too much pain. Then suddenly, the spirit will emerge through the lives of ordinary people who hear a call and answer in extraordinary ways.

Mother Teresa

~

I wondered how well nurses in Australia would cope with such a task in such poverty, and whether they would approach the person with such an open heart and such a beautiful smile. *'We shall never know all the good that a simple smile can do.'* (Mother Teresa 2003).

Despite all the problems in Calcutta, it is a city with a soul. Survival has become a creative art, yet the Calcuttans themselves are the happiest bunch of people in the country. There was not once that I gave a smile and did not receive one back, even if it was with tremendous effort. I remember an elderly lady who was dying, lying on the floor on a mattress in the foetal position, extremely weak, but she lifted her head as I came past, held her hands together slowly, and whispered 'Namaste'. This consumed all her energy but somehow she managed. When lowering her head back onto the pillow, she had the most beautiful smile; there was something angelic about her. Several hours later she died.

The simple gestures of a kind touch, assisting with a sponge bath, feeding, pain relief, or lovingly cradling a person so that the last thing they witnessed before dying was the face of love were all in day's. Work at Kalighat.

It took me a long time to settle down when I came back to Australia. Physically and mentally I was back in Australia, but spiritually I was still in Calcutta.

I will always have a special place in my heart for Kalighat, and will continue to personally pray to Mother Teresa for her intercessory prayer and guidance for my work with the dying. As Mother Teresa states *"We are all only a pencil in God's hand and it he writes and he who tell the story"*.

~

We cannot all do great things, but we can do small things with great love.
Mother Teresa, personal communication, (1980)

~

23

Dona Di Maria Home: Here I Am, Lord

Having spent time at Mother Teresa home for the Dying in Calcutta, I was really excited about doing some volunteer work at another one of her homes, this time in Rome. What an adventure to reach my destination! The home was situated outside the Vatican wall at St Peters Square; therefore I had to obtain permission from the Swiss guards to enter. This was eventually given and I was on my way. As I approached the large green doors to the home, I was very excited, until I knocked on the door and an extremely aggressive nun answered – she was screaming, and part of me wanted to run for the hills. However, I was rescued by one of the most angelic faces I have ever seen.

It was arranged that I would return the next morning at 6am to assist the Sisters in preparing food for the women who came daily for a warm and nutritious lunch. These were women and young girls who lived on the street. It was hard to comprehend, that within the richness of the city of Rome with its wonderful buildings such as the Vatican, Sistine Chapel, and magnificent churches and cathedrals, such poverty existed.

The next morning I was a little apprehensive due to the reception of the night before, but all night I had a song going through my head, *Should I go or should I stay*, over and over. I knew that I had to go.

By the time I approached those large doors again, my heart was pounding with excitement. As I rang the doorbell three times I quietly prayed for strength and courage to step into the unknown. 'Here I am Lord', I said to myself as I rang the bell.

As I helped the Sisters to prepare the meals for the homeless and destitute, I felt so humbled. This was an amazing experience and I could not help but think of Mother Teresa's words, *In the poor we see Jesus*. As I stood there cutting tomatoes, the Sisters and two volunteers began to sing, *Here I am Lord*. I was amazed and started to cry as this is my favourite hymn and one which is symbolic of my work. As I glanced out the window there was a beautiful statue of the Virgin Mary, just looking at me as if to say, 'You are where you are meant to be, all is well'.

The Sisters were amazing; many of them were very thin, yet they were able to lift huge pots of soup. Everything was done with so much joy, singing hymns of praise the whole time. When the Sisters smiled, their whole faces reflected their love of Jesus and the Virgin Mary. One of the Sisters had come from the Mother House in Calcutta, so we had an immediate bond. The whole time that I worked there, the Sisters called me 'Therese'.

Parmesan cheese (real Italian!) needed to be hand-grated. As it was past its 'use by' date, it needed to be fermented so it could be used. Forty large pieces of cheese later, with blisters on my hands and several cuts, I had completed the task of grating the cheese. This task was followed by cutting the red surrounding wax into small pieces as this was then melted and also used for various purposes.

Nothing was wasted. I helped prepare minestrone soup, pasta, salad, bread rolls, tea and coffee plus three platters of fried fish for the evening meal. Lunch time arrived, and approximately 25 women of all ages entered into the dining room for their meal. Each one of these women had a unique story of why they needed assistance. Before the eating, grace was said, and each person in the room bowed their head in thanks and praise and there was much thanks also given to Mother Teresa.

One young girl was only 16 and was living on the streets, homeless, and four months pregnant. Her family had disowned her when she became pregnant and she had nowhere to go. As I was giving out the bread rolls to accompany the soup she begged me for another, when the Sisters were not looking – naturally I gave it to her. There was such desperation in her eyes, that I could not ignore this request. Each woman there was so grateful for the assistance that the Sisters gave them each day, one meal a day – but a hearty meal. One lady was 50 years old, and spoke very good English. She shared with me that she had HIV, and not only did the Sisters give her food each day, but brought her the medication required for this disease. As I looked into her eyes, there was a spark, unusual for one so sick, she was so alive. 'I put all my trust in Our Lady', she quietly whispered to me, 'She led me here, and she will be there when I die'. She told me that she had no fear of dying, but only being alone when it occurred. The Sisters quickly reassured her that she would not be alone when the time eventually came.

Each one of these ladies and young girls had a story to tell, a story of human survival, of despair, sadness and rejection. But the one thread which they all shared was that of faith and hope.

My time at Dona Di Maria was such a rich, humbling experience, a true blessing. The Sisters, were so devoted in serving the poor of Rome, and their faces all shone with God's love, continually giving unconditional love to all who entered those large green doors – including volunteers from Australia.

~

Let us touch the dying, the poor, the lonely and the unwanted according to the graces we have received and let us not be ashamed or slow to do the humble work.

Mother Teresa

~

Hail Mary

Hail Mary, full of grace.

The Lord is with thee.

Blessed art thou amongst women,

and blessed is the fruit of thy womb, Jesus.

Holy Mary, Mother of God,

pray for us sinners,

now and at the hour of our death.

Amen.

Catholic Prayer

24

Anne: Can I Go Now?

Anne was 89 years of age and originally from Ireland. She had been a prominent character in the local community for many years. During this period, Anne had donated countless hours to community services and charities. She had been friends with my grandmother for many years; Nan spoke about her with warm affection.

Anne was an extremely spiritual lady; she attended the church regularly throughout her life, and she had a deep faith which she practised daily. We would have amazing conversations about death and dying and the angels. Anne believed she had a special relationship with the angels and would communicate with them regularly. She had a deep insight into the lives of the other residents and would know exactly when an old soul was going to 'the light'.

Anne's health began to deteriorate quite rapidly. She was having frequent transient ischaemic attacks, each episode lasting longer and leaving her with some physical deficits. At times the attacks were so severe that I did not think she would survive.

Eventually, she had a stroke. This left her with severe paralysis down the left side of her body requiring full nursing care with all her activities.

As her health continued to deteriorate, Anne became incontinent of urine. This distressed her terribly – she longed to go to heaven. She was so tired and had had enough; she would often express that she was ready to die, but God would not come and get her and she was becoming impatient. The physical body was more than ready to leave, but still the spirit was strong; the timing not quite right.

Anne understood and believed that one does not go to heaven before that exact moment that the spirit is meant to leave, but even so she longed to 'go home'.

Over the next few months Anne experienced another major stroke, and it was clear that she was not going to recover – she was dying. Anne also knew this, but there was no fear, just relief. 'At last!' she said. As her condition deteriorated I sat quietly by her bed, holding her hand, reading her favourite verses from the Bible. The music in the background at Anne's *request was not solemn, but that of celebration and rejoicing – Gospel music* – 'Oh Happy Day'. While her old Bible was tightly clasped in her hand, with her small silver cross hanging gently around her neck, suddenly her old tired eyes connected with mine, and there was a smile in those eyes, a sparkle of hope, showing her true spirit. 'May I go now?' She enquired, requesting the permission she needed. 'Of course you can', I said softly. With that she smiled and said, 'God is here now'. She squinted her eyes. 'The light is so bright, I have never seen anything so beautiful.' Gently I replied, 'Go to the light Anne, it is okay, God has you a place in heaven.' At that exact moment there was also the most beautiful feeling of serenity in the room, and God's presence was so real that it was evident to both of us. 'Will you please stay with me until I leave?' she asked. I placed my arms around her, cradling her with love, gently singing 'Oh Happy Day'. Within a few minutes, quietly and effortlessly Anne took her last breath surrendering into the light, leaving behind her tired old body, her spirit soaring upwards on an amazing journey back to her creator.

~

My soul is awakened my spirit is soaring, and carried aloft on the wings of the breeze.

Anne Bronte

~

25

Eunice: Untangling the Knots

It was Monday morning, 8am on an exceptionally cold winter's day. As I approached the nurses' station an extremely thin, frail elderly lady, slowly entered the room. Her clothing, was in tatters, an old skirt, barely covering her knobby knees, her blouse was missing several buttons, grey in color, jumper to match with holes all through it. The stench of her clothing was over whelming. She appeared as if she had not had a shower for months, her personal hygiene was non existent. She wore a tattered blue hat, which was made from felt, but it too was in ruins. What had happened to this old soul? How had she been so neglected by society?

Eunice was 92 years of age, and had been living alone in her home, without any assistance. It was not until recently that the local council had intervened and arranged for her to have some emergency respite care in the aged care facility where I was working. She had no family, and no friends to speak of, she lived what appeared to be a very isolated and lonely life.

In speaking to Eunice and establishing her medical records it was discovered that she had not only had dementia but advanced bowel cancer which had metastasised throughout her body, her prognosis was extremely poor. Looking deeply into her old eyes, I could clearly see that she was dying.

As I approached her gently, with compassion very slowly she glanced up at me timidly. Her piercing blue eyes penetrated my heart with such warmth, and gratitude. There was something extremely special about this old lady – a light from within one could even say angelic. For some reason, she would not permit any other staff member to come near her, and became extremely frightened and distressed when attempted. Therefore, I became Eunice's nurse for the coming week. After much encouragement and gentle persuasion, Eunice agreed to me giving her a long overdue shower. This was to be a tremendous task for both nurse and patient.

As I removed her old hat, I was shocked to discover the thickness of her grey hair which was rolled up in a bun on the top of her head, suspended with two rusted hair pins. It was not only unclean, but had a terrible odour and was completely mattered. One could not even put a comb through it. The hairdresser of the facility came in to see what she could do and quickly recommended that it all should all be cut off.

When this was suggested Eunice broke into tears, pleading for her hair not to be cut, stating that it was the only thing that made her feel pretty – she was so distressed, it broke my heart to see such a beautiful old soul, crying as the hairdresser threatened her with the scissors.

She stared up at me with so much hope and tears in her eyes, like a child looking to their mother to intervene for protection to stop this from occurring. With this I convinced the hairdresser to please let me attempt to get the matter out – to give it a go at least!

To this the hairdresser muttered "Impossible".

"Nothing is impossible when you believe in God" Eunice said, nothing. Smiling warmly at me as though she had just won a victory.

I was determined to work on Eunice's hair before her shower as I realized that it was going to take a long time for this almost impossible task. My friend who was a hair dresser suggested that I use several bottles of baby oil to assist to detangle the hair, before trying to wash in the shower. This was going to be a time-consuming process, requiring extensive patience, but I was determined to succeed, as

Eunice's hair was so important to her, and a key element in caring for her spirit. Using a large wide tooth comb we commenced what would prove to be a four hour progression of detangling the hair. As I glanced at the large bucket of hair which had been removed, I to felt a certain triumph.

Then it was off to the shower. Gently I assisted Eunice to remove her old clothes. They were so filthy, that parts of her blouse had to be soaked off her skin with soap, as the fibers imbedded into her skin. As I lathered the soap onto her body, she was overjoyed with the beautiful fragrance of the lavender. She was in pure heaven. I then applied the shampoo followed by a deep condition, which I combed through her hair without any tangles at all.

After drying Eunice after her shower I applied lavender powder and deodorant, two items which she had not used for many months. Once again she delighted in the pure aroma of the fragrances. I then assisted her to get dressed – a blue floral dress which had been handed into lost and found, with matching blue cardigan, underwear and slippers. Eunice was in awe of her new outfit.

Next was the hairdryer, with a complete blow wave. Eunice's long grey hair was now shinning, clean and looking beautiful, one could hardly recognise the long perfectly groomed mane as the tangled mattered hair that previously encountered. As I assisted her to the mirror her face lit up with Joy, the spark returning into her eyes.

During our time together, she spoke of dying without any fear or distress, expressing that she had a deep faith in God, and prayed daily. She was extremely spiritual and would often speak of encounters with angels throughout her life.

During various periods of her life when she was at her lowest it were the angels who she would rely on to give her love and comfort, so that she was never alone. She then whispered quietly in my ear, that she had prayed to God that she would be taken to a hospital where she did not have to die alone. And yes, God had heard her prayers, and here she was. She then added with such conviction in her voice that she would be returning home to God by the end of the week.

For the next four days, this delightful old lady radiated pure love to all those who crossed her path. Staff hardly recognised her as the same old lady who had presented only five days ago. She was beautifully dressed, hair was striking, worn down for all to admire-her spirit was so alive, her eyes radiated genuine bliss, while her character and charm touched all those who cared for her.

On the Friday morning, Eunice asked me if I could wash her hair and blow dry it for the last time as she wanted it to look beautiful when she came face to face with God. Naturally, I did as she asked. During the shower, Eunice shared with me the most beautiful story of the angel who had visited her the night before, describing in such detail the beauty and radiance of the being. The light around her was so bright that I could hardly look she stated, the light was radiating all around the room. The angel told her that she would be returning home to God on Friday night.

Before I left for the day, Eunice called me in to her room, embracing me, thanking me for all my care and love, and for taking the time to untangle her hair. She said that in life dear there were often situations that may be "Tangled", and may take time to work through, but with God's help and prayer that all is possible. She expressed that she had experienced more love and laughter in that one week than she had for over 20 years, that God had placed her in the right place for the end of her life and beginning of her Journey-back to the light. As I kissed her goodbye on her cheek, I could feel my tears gently touch her face, as I knew in my heart that she was about to embark on her final journey.

Sure enough, that night, in the small hours of the morning, Eunice died peacefully in her sleep, her silver white hair beautifully groomed as she was escorted by the angels back to her Creator in heaven.

~

If we make our goal to live a life of compassion and unconditional love,
Then the world will indeed become a garden
Where all kinds of flowers can bloom and grow.

Elisabeth Külber Ross (1926 – 2004)

~

26

Sam: The Yellow Rose

Sam was one of the most inspirational and courageous women I have ever had the privilege of nursing. She was only 50 years of age when she was diagnosed with metastatic breast cancer. Although she had tried all the available cancer treatments, nothing had been successful, so she decided to 'live life to the fullest' for as long as she could. 'It may not be a long time, but it will be a great time.'

Sam came from a close and loving family. Her parents, siblings, husband and two children visited her daily, and she was extremely loved. For one who was dying, I had never met someone so alive. To Sam, each day was a blessing from God. She was an extremely spiritual person, who had explored many avenues along her journey with cancer, particularly finding comfort in meditation and prayer.

Sam had worked as a primary school teacher and was devoted to her students, many of whom would visit her while she was in hospital – teaching was her passion. Sam and I developed an instant spiritual connection the first moment we met, and it was this connection of grace that would guide me with Sam's care until her final journey.

During the two years I nursed Sam, I got to know both her and the family very well. I was continually amazed by her fighting spirit and courage. We would spend a lot of time discussing God, heaven, angels, spirit and her love of her family. Many times she expressed that she had no fear of dying, and was getting very tired of the continual battle for physical existence. Then one day I heard her say in her prayer, 'I surrender, your will be done.'

Eventually Sam was discharged from hospital to go home. She

loved the garden and, in particular, yellow roses which were the pride and joy. The garden was her sanctuary, a place of peace, where she could be still, contemplate and, most importantly, talk to God.

At much the same time, I left the hospital and commenced home nursing, and once again our paths crossed on a community-based palliative care program. On Christmas Eve that year, there was a knock at my front door, and when I answered it, there was Sam, still attached to her syringe driver with morphine, bald from all the chemotherapy, thin and frail, but with the most beautiful smile that could only be described as 'angelic', her eyes sparkling, reflecting the spirit within. Somehow she had found out my address, and she delivered me the most beautiful hand-embroidered pillow, which she had made for me for Christmas. I was overcome, immediately invited her in for a Christmas drink. I will always treasure that pillow and the love and courage that it represents.

For the next months I visited Sam weekly on a professional basis. One weekend while I was at a friend's wedding, I suddenly had an overwhelming feeling that Sam needed me – it was like an angel tapping me on the shoulder, telling me to go. I left the wedding and immediately went to the hospital. The feeling or 'inner knowing' was so strong that I did not even phone her home or her family, I just arrived. When I entered her room, she quietly said to me, 'I have been waiting for you', tears welling up in her eyes. Even then, so weak and tired, Sam was still encouraging me to specialise in palliative care. 'You will be shown', she confidently said. This was one goodbye that was going to be extremely difficult for me and would affect me in many ways both professionally and personally. I spent several hours with Sam, before saying our last goodbye. Sam died that night with her family by her side. They gave me a special gift – time to spend with their precious Sam, to speak to her, to pray with her and for her, and to give her all my love.

At Sam's funeral I was given a single yellow rose. I placed it in a pretty vase with her order of service behind it. There was no breeze in the room, yet when I had returned, several petals of the rose had fallen from the vase and onto my application for further studies in palliative care.

~

Take a minute of your lifetime
to enjoy a pretty bloom,
Pick a rose from nature's garden,
It will brighten up your room.

Be not haste in all your doings,
as you hurry through the day,
But enjoy what God gives freely;
Smell the roses while you may.

Bill Carr

~

27

Boris: The Conductor

Boris was a 92-year-old man, originally from Russia. He spoke little English, and this was also complicated by his cognitive decline due to dementia. Consequently, communication was exceedingly difficult. Even interpreters found it extremely hard to communicate with this dear old man. Boris had the most piercing blue eyes, which would light up with joy when he was approached by staff members. Each visit I would say to him, 'Good morning handsome', and his face would light up and he would giggle.

Boris loved music, and would spend his time listening to it, especially to the Philharmonic Orchestra, which he belonged to for over 50 years. Boris was a conductor in Europe.

Boris had lived through World War II, serving as a soldier with the Russian army. He had never married, or had a family. Visitors were few; his room was small quite bare, not homely at all, with only an odd photo here and there portraying both his time in the army and his musical life throughout the world.

Over the following months Boris was diagnosed with aggressive bowel cancer which had metastasised to his liver; he was dying. Each week, when I came to visit Boris, I felt so sad that he had no other visitors; the room was dark, with no colour, not even his music playing. He was just lying there waiting to die. The staff at this facility had no idea about palliative care.

As I was walking out of the room one day, I went over to his CD player and selected a CD, bringing the player up to his bed so that he could hear it. The music started, and even though he was drifting in and out of consciousness, something within his spirit connected with that music. I stood in the doorway just watching this beautiful old man, so weak and frail, but somehow, he lifted his old arms up into the air, and began to once again, and for the last time, conduct to the music. As I approached him I could see that his eyes were wide open, and full of tears which were running down his old cheeks. I wondered what he was imagining as he continued to conduct in time with the music – was he back in Russia, in front of a live audience at a grand concert, standing in the front of the orchestra dressed in the black tuxedo suit and bow tie as pictured in his photos? Wherever he was travelling, and whatever he was seeing, he was in awe. He continually repeated the word 'Ahren, Ahren' as well as 'ohhh, ohhh' as if he had just seen something so beautiful. His old face said it all; there was a beautiful look of serenity and amazement, and also of joy. I wondered what those words meant; there was no-one around to ask, but I sensed that it was something sacred. At the same time there was a beautiful feeling within the room; I was sure that God's presence was there, and I felt in my heart that Boris was also seeing God – being given that little glimpse of heaven, which often those who are dying are shown just before they transcend.

Boris continued conducting, arms up in the air for the whole of the CD, and when it was finished he gently placed his arms down by his side, looked at me and said, 'Болото Bog Ljubit Vas, Ahren'. At exactly the same time as these words were spoken a Russian volunteer entered the room, and told me what he had said. 'Thank you, God loves you … Angel'. These beautiful words were uttered from a man who was dying, a man who never spoke, yet somehow through the cloud of mysticism he was able to give me such a beautiful parting gift.

Placing his old hands softly on his chest, and gently closing his weary eyes, Boris drifted off peacefully to the heavenly realm, where

I am sure he is conducting a choir of angels for the glory of God.

~

You are the Music while the Music lasts.

T.S. Elliot

~

28

Myrtle: Over the Rainbow

Myrtle was 95 years of age, and was diagnosed with advanced breast cancer which had metastasised into various other organs. Our paths first crossed when I was requested to review her pain management regimen. From our first encounter we developed a special bond, one which would continue for the next five months until she died.

Myrtle was an extremely spiritual lady, and had experienced many supernatural events throughout her life. She loved to speak of God, the angels and heaven, and she believed in the power of prayer. She was a beautiful old soul, but so tired and longing to go 'home' to be reunited once again with her husband. She had a very supportive and loving family who visited her daily.

One night I had the most vivid dream. Myrtle was standing on the end of the most beautiful coloured double rainbow, the colours were radiant, red, blue, pink, purple, green and gold all reflecting glorious beams of light. At the other end of the rainbow there was a young man, with fair hair, piercing blue eyes and a beautiful warm smile. He was dressed in a tweed suit, with a hat to match, and he wore a red rose on his lapel. As I looked at this figure I noted that the thumb on his right hand was missing.

I wondered what had occurred; obviously he was in an accident. I did not recognise him, and Myrtle did not have any photos displayed in her room except for several of her grandchildren.

The next week when I went to see Myrtle I shared with her about the beautiful dream which I had, as I knew in my heart that I was being led to do so. With tears in her eyes, she looked at me and asked me to get a small box from the drawer. She opened the box to reveal a photo of her wedding day. There was the young man who I had seen in my dream; he was her husband Harry. And, yes, he had a thumb missing. Myrtle explained to me that he used to work in a factory with machinery and that is how he lost his thumb. As we sat speaking of the amazing gift which we had both been given, I glanced out the window as the sky was becoming overcast and there was a double rainbow in all its splendour.

From that moment on, the symbol of the rainbow became very important in Myrtle's final journey home to God.

The next day that I came in to see Myrtle, her grandson was with her. As I entered the room, he began to play his guitar and softly sing to his grandmother, *Somewhere over the rainbow*. Myrtle had not shared the dream with anyone at that stage.

Eventually, Myrtle's condition deteriorated. She was dying. As I entered the room, she spoke of the rainbow in all its splendour, stating that she could see her husband waiting for her, 'It is so beautiful.' During the next few hours Myrtle also spoke of the glorious white light – 'luminescent' was the word she used to describe its brilliance – it was soaking into her soul, and drawing her home.

'Can you please open the curtains so that I can see the sky?' She asked as if she was being directed to do so. As I opened the curtains there once again was a beautiful double rainbow. 'My rainbow', she said, 'There it is.' Myrtle then whispered to me, 'Whenever you see a rainbow I will be watching over you.' In the early hours of the morning, Myrtle died peacefully, surrounded by her family.

Naturally I attended her funeral. After it was finished I was anxious to get home as the sky was becoming dark and it looked like rain. However, on my way home, my car overheated, forcing me to stop on the side of the road. What a place to break down, I thought, but it turned out to be the most perfect place. As I sat there waiting for the RACV to come and assist, I glanced into the sky and there in all its glory was, yet again, the most beautiful coloured double rainbow, just coming over the surrounding hills. At that moment I knew that Myrtle was 'watching over me'.

~

When it looked like the sun wasn't going to shine any more, there's a rainbow in the clouds.

Maya Angelou

~

29

Sister Angelica: The Rosary Beads

Over the years I have been blessed to have known and cared for such extraordinary people, all with their own unique story to tell, all of whom have played an intricate role in my own spiritual journey.

While working in a Catholic nursing home, I met the most beautiful nun – Sister Angelica. She belonged to the Good Samaritan order. Over the year in which I cared for Sister Angelica, she took it upon herself to introduce me into the Catholic faith, and was indeed a catalyst for my later conversion into Catholicism. Sister Angelica had been a teacher all her life, so at the appropriate time she decided with absolute certainty that she should teach me the Holy Rosary. I thought this was a wonderful idea as I had always been very drawn to the Virgin Mary, and in this way I could learn more about the Catholic faith. Each day I would spend time with Sister Angelica as she patiently, with such deep devotion, taught me each decade of the rosary. It took me a long while to learn, and there was much celebration in the end with 'By George she has got it. Hooray, Hooray'.

A few months later Sister Angelica declined in health, and I eventually was asked by the other nuns to be her palliative care nurse. This was indeed an honour. I spent many hours with her privately during this period. She expressed much joy when I confidently recited the Holy Rosary which she had taught me, following each decade on her own old beads. During this time she shared amazing stories of faith, love and service for Jesus and the Virgin Mary. Her life had been one of fullness; she had devoted her whole life to service, both as a Good Samaritan Sister and as a teacher. At times she would ask me to read her favourite passages from the Bible, while she continued to hold firmly onto her much loved rosary beads. These rosaries were over 80 years old and were her prized possession; it is difficult to imagine all the prayers that those beads would have endured over the years through the trials and tribulations of life. They were well worn and well used, and immensely sacred. Sister Angelica held them tightly clasped to her chest up to the moment of her death.

After Sister Angelica died, I assisted one of the Sisters to prepare her for her final journey home. I was invited to Sister Angelica's Vigil Mass. It was absolutely beautiful. The procession of candles from those present, lighting the way into the chapel was like a scene from a medieval movie, from hundreds of years ago. The beautiful light and quietness was accompanied with a real feel of serenity.

As the procession filtered into the chapel, I was amazed at how many people were there, nuns, priests, family, friends, nurses. In the middle of the altar lay Sister Angelica in her casket. As the procession passed by, I realised that it was an open casket. As I looked down at my dear old friend/teacher, I could not help but think how angelic she looked. She was dressed in her full habit, with her rosary beads, in her clasped hands over her chest. She seemed to have a gentle smile on her face. What had she seen? Something beautiful I'm sure.

The Reverend Mother then commenced the Mass, speaking of Sister Angelica's life, and all those who she had touched over her lifetime; her impact on people, particularly students, had been remarkable. She was a teacher right up to the end.

The Reverend Mother then asked if anyone would like to speak of their relationship with Sister Angelica, and almost before I realised it, I stood up, in a room full of strangers and began to speak of my relationship with this beautiful old nun. On reflection, I now realise that it was the Holy Spirit which made me stand up, I just knew I had to; I had such heat in my heart, and became shaky, not because of nerves, but because of the spiritual energy of the Holy Spirit. From where I was standing I could clearly see Sister Angelica, and it seemed that she had a look on her face as if to say, 'Well done, the first step into Catholicism'.

After I had finished speaking, the Reverend Mother came over to me and presented me with Sister Angelica's rosary beads as she felt that I should have them as I had learnt the rosary on them and this was Sister Angelica's wish. I was overcome with emotion, could not stop crying, and cannot, even now, express the feeling of such love in my heart. This was one of the most beautiful spiritual events of my life.

The next day I returned for the funeral, and was amazed to see that from all the flowers which were brought for Sister Angelica, it was my pink roses that were kept by her side all night during the vigil. Yet no-one knew that I had brought them, no-one, except God of course. At the end of the service a very little old nun in her late 90s approached me with a small box and said, 'When I was given my first rosary beads dear, a little old nun like myself gave me a small box like this one, so I would like to give this one to you to keep your special rosary beads in.' As Sister Angelica left, once again the pink roses were the ones which were dominant on her casket. I could not help but smile to myself and give thanks for such a special nun, who was used by heaven to start me on my amazing journey into the Catholic faith.

~

Flowers are God's way of smiling.

Anon

~

30

Harold: Jesus Don't Forget Me

Harold was 95 years of age, and lived in the facility where I was working. He was diagnosed with advanced dementia and various other medical conditions which were a natural part of the ageing process.

Harold had a strong faith, and one which he liked to share with others. He would continually speak of his visits with the 'angels', and how beautiful they were, finding it difficult to describe their beauty he would simply say they were 'heavenly in every sense'. Because of his dementia, Harold's cognitive state fluctuated; at times he was quite confused and disorientated to time, place and person, and would try to abscond from the facility, while on other occasions he was lucid and quiet sharp. He was quite clever in his plans of 'escape' and would have the timing of absconding perfect. He had a wonderful sense of humour, and always had a joke or two up his sleeve to share with the staff.

Early one morning, dressed in his best pyjamas, dressing gown, blue slippers, and bowler hat, Harold absconded from the facility with only a few gold coins in his pocket. He walked to the local train station to catch transport into Melbourne's central area to attend a church service at St. Paul's Cathedral. The adventure into the city on the train would have taken at least 45 minutes, but for some reason no-one seemed to notice this dear old soul sitting quietly in his night attire. Meanwhile, back at the facility the police had been called, and the fact that Harold had dementia increased their concern. Harold was oblivious to all the fuss that he was creating and sat quietly in the church listening to the service, singing at the top of his voice to all the hymns. It was not until Communion that the Minister noticed that one of his flock was dressed in his pyjamas, thus alerting him to the fact that something was wrong. On further inspection, he noticed Harold's ID bracelet, his name, place of residence and phone number. With this the Minister asked, ' Why have you come all this way?' 'I want to make sure that Jesus has not forgotten me.' To this the Minister replied, 'The Lord will never forget you Harold.' 'Well', Harold gently replied, 'I am going home to heaven very soon, so I want to make sure that Jesus knows that I am coming, so that I do not lose my way. You see, the angels come all the time, and they are beautiful, and they are coming to get me soon. This is the cathedral where I was married over 60 years ago, so I wanted to come here, to remind Jesus that I am a child of God, and am waiting to go home.' With this the Minister felt his eyes well up with tears, 'Be not afraid Harold, the Lord will be with you.' After this very clear and lucid conversation, Harold became disorientated and confused. It appeared that he had been given this special gift of clarity for a short period to fulfil his mission and share such beautiful words with the Minister.

Not long after this, the police arrived to escort Harold back to the facility. When he arrived, the staff were thrilled to see him, giving him hug after hug, which he responded to with joy. As I embraced this beautiful old soul, I could see this spark in his eyes, which had previously not been present; the eyes which were once distant were now alive with spirit. I knew that something had transpired at the church, but did not find out what until the following day.

As I assisted Harold into bed, he once again appeared to have a short period of clarity. 'Jesus is coming tonight and I am going home', he stated so confidently to me. Witnessing the spark in his eyes I agreed with him and said, 'Yes Harold, I think that you are right. Be not afraid', I said to him without realising that he had already heard this same thing once before today from the Minister. 'That is what the

Minister said to me today', he said, and then shared with me all that had occurred on his adventure to the cathedral.

Before I left the room, I kissed Harold on the cheek. 'Until we meet again dear Harold may God hold you in the palm of his hand' 'Yes dear, God Bless you.'

That night Harold was escorted to heaven, quietly and peacefully without any fuss – he was home.

Irish Blessing

May the road rise up to meet you
May the winds always be at you back.
May the sun shine warm upon your face.
And rain fall soft upon your fields.
And until we meet again.
May God hold you in the palm of his hand.

Author unknown

31

Maria: The Brown Scapular

One evening I was cleaning out a drawer in my dressing table when I came across what they call a 'brown scapular' – this consists of a brown piece of blessed cloth on a string. It is an important symbol in the Catholic faith, particularly with older generations. Catholics wear the brown scapular around their necks when they are dying. My friend had brought it back from Medjugorje.

The next morning I went to work and was sent out to organise an admission. When I reached the home I was greeted by a lovely old lady, Maria, and her daughter. We seemed to have an immediate connection. Maria was from Bosnia Herzegovina-Medjugorje, a place where I intended to travel to towards the end of the year. When I shared this with her, her tired old eyes lit up with joy as she proudly told me of her homeland. 'There is only one thing I want and need for my death', she stated to me, 'Would you be able to bring me one back if I am still alive?' Yes, it was a brown scapular. There was silence, and I just looked at her in amazement as I knew that there would be someone who would like that brown scapular, but the next day? How often the Holy Spirit directs us to cross paths with another at the exact time that we are needed. The timing of these connections is perfect and there is no mistake of its intention.

The next time I visited her I gave her the scapular. It was as if I had given her the world, her old eyes filling up with tears of joy as she said; 'Now I am prepared for my journey home.'

~

'Joy is a light that fills you with faith, hope and love'
Adela Rogers

I must admit that I felt intensely moved and privileged to be part of that very special moment. Maria had such a devout faith; there was no fear, just acceptance – she was tired and ready to go to heaven. She had daily visits from her priest of many years for Holy Communion, which gave her much comfort. Maria would spend the rest of her day reading the Bible. Over the next few months her condition declined. The changing face of hope was no longer for a 'miracle' cure, but for that of a peaceful death, to be gently escorted home by the angels, and to be reunited with her beloved husband.

She died three months later, with the scapular safely around her neck. As I was on leave I did not know until I returned to work. I felt upset that I was not given the opportunity to say 'goodbye', nor have the opportunity for some 'closure', as the journey with Maria and her family had been very special.

The day after finding out that she had died, my friend asked me to go to Mass with her, which I did. After Communion, I had to walk up the back of the church to get to my seat. There on the floor in the middle of the aisle was an open book. I picked it up and read what was on the page – 'The importance of the brown scapular'. I nearly fell over backwards. In that instant the circle of care of Maria felt complete, and I knew in my heart that all was well.

Whispering Hope

Soft as the voice of an angel,
Breathing a lesson unheard,
Hope with a gentle persuasion,
Whispers her comforting word:

Wait till the darkness is over,
Wait till the tempest is done,
Hope for the sunshine tomorrow,
After the shower is gone.

Septimus Winner

32

Liza: The Prayer Chair and the Butterfly

Liza (a pseudonym we used for her) was now 65 years of age, and was a well established actress in the entertainment industry. Liza had advanced breast cancer which had metastasised into her bowel, and her prognosis was poor. As a palliative care nurse, we enter into our patient's home; we are usually invited to travel that Journey with those who are dying and their families. Nurses and Health care professionals are a lot like Ministers, Priests or Nuns in a way, as patients often share their inner most thoughts, wishes and regrets which are too deep, or difficult to share with their families.

As with all those who have come under my care over the years trust and integrity, as well as confidentiality and respect were even more imperative when caring for a well know "Celebrity". Not only did I have to care for Liza but also with the Media who were present each day, trying to establish her condition.

Liza's house faced onto the ocean, this was her haven and what nurtured her spirit. Each afternoon until early evening she would sit in her "prayer", chair and meditate and prayer, reciting the holy rosary and she fingered each bead with such devotion. With the crashing of the waves as they came into shore, she would breathe the sea air in and exhale with gratitude. Her prayer chair was her favorite possession. It was a large white chair which was decorated with floral cushions, at times she would sleep in it on a warm summer evening. This chair was one of the first items she brought when she became famous, it was also her favorite. As far as Liza was concerned you could keep the Limos, hired help, helicopters, and flash houses, all she needed was her beautiful chair. Regularly, each time that Liza would sit in her prayer chair a butterfly, would come and land on her shoulder, or the side of her chair, once even hovering over the pocket of her tracksuit near her heart. She loved butterflies, and would often tell me that soon she too would be free like a butterfly, and soaring up into the heavens. Liza expressed that she had no fear of death, that in actual fact it would be a welcome relief, as she was so tired and longed to return home to her Creator.

~

Happiness is a butterfly, which when pursued, is always just beyond your grasp, but which, if you sit down quietly, may alight upon you.

Nathaniel Hawthorne

~

Each evening as it was balmy I would take Liza out to the veranda and assist her from her wheel chair into her "prayer chair". Her condition was quickly deteriorating, she was becoming so weak each day an effort. Yet, when she was seated in her prayer chair, surrounded by her beautiful cushions, with a light pink crochet rug over her knees it provided her with so much Joy and comfort, much like a cocoon embracing a beautiful butterfly.

It was Liza's wish if possible to die in her beautiful chair; she had no real family as fame had created wedges too deep to heal. It broke my heart that she had no one. I had the privilege to care for such a beautiful human being, and the spirit of that person, had really touched my heart, yet when it came to her death, who would be here?

So with God's help and the angels I was determined to make her one request come true.

As the sun gently rose over the water Liza quietly called me over to her side, kissing me on the cheek, and thanked me for my care and for walking beside her along her journey. She then whispered in my ear that whenever I see a butterfly to think of her as she will be watching over me from heaven. She then winked at me, giving me the most angelic smile, and as the waves came crashing down onto the shore, took her final breath.

After Liza's body was taken, I shut the door behind me as I walked out onto the veranda for the last time and there resting on the prayer chair in all its glory was the most beautiful brown and orange butterfly – she was free.

~

We delight in the beauty of the butterfly, but rarely admit the changes it has gone through to achieve that beauty.

Maya Angelou

~

33

Mavis: The "Queen Mother"

This story occurred many years ago, but has always remained in my heart.

It unfolded on an oncology ward at a Melbourne-based hospital where I had been working for approximately 12 months. During this time I had the privilege of having nursed, known and cared for some of the most amazing and courageous people that I have ever had the honour of meeting.

Mavis was no exception. She was 88 years of age when she was diagnosed with cancer, so she was regularly admitted to hospital for treatment. She lived with her daughter Betty and they shared a very close relationship. She also had an particularly close family network, consisting of children, grandchildren, and great grandchildren, and she also had many friends.

When Mavis was first admitted into the hospital we developed an immediate bond. I affectionately gave her the nickname 'The Queen Mother', because when she would walk down the corridor with the aid of her walking frame all had to clear the way – she was coming through. She was a real lady, little and petite, beautifully groomed, and of the old school; she also possessed a wicked sense of humour.

Over the months of her treatment, we shared many special moments discussing those topics which I consider it an honour to discuss with others. Although tears were shed at times, there was also much joyous laughter. The special time spent together gave Mavis the opportunity in a safe, trusting environment to express negative emotions, to pray, and to tie up loose ends. She had a deep devotion and strong faith, which was demonstrated in her courageous fight for life.

Mavis, like many other patients, enjoyed lavender aromatic massages, which I gave her regularly as part of her pain management, and as requested by her family. She stated on each occasion that she greatly looked forward to this time and she could not believe how much comfort she derived from the gentle touch and nurturing that a relaxation massage provided. 'Touch is one of the most important things a nurse can give a patient', she said. The aroma of the lavender oil prompted her to reminisce about her childhood, and this then led her to speak of matters of the heart. Mavis's health eventually began to deteriorate rapidly. She was moved to a private room and her family summoned. She was in liver failure – her system was shutting down. The oncologist, stony faced and grim but emotionless, bluntly stated to the family that Mavis did not have much longer to live and then briskly turned and walked out of the room, leaving the family traumatised. When they eventually recovered their composure, they asked if I could give Mavis one last aromatic massage as she loved the aroma of the lavender oil and the gentle touch. At this stage she was drifting in and out of consciousness. As I began the massage both Betty and I could sense the most amazing sense of serenity and a gentle presence so real that it was almost palpable. Her daughter, Betty, continued to pray for her mother as I was massaging her. I was very aware of the love being projected to Mavis through the prayer of her daughter and other family members. The fragrance of the lavender oil hung gently in the air and there was a quiet stillness all around. On placing my hands on Mavis's frail body, I became aware of the change in her energy and I felt that she would soon be leaving to go on her journey back to god.

At one point while holding Mavis' hand, I thought that she had quietly died, but then suddenly she opened her eyes and looked straight into mine and said, 'There is beautiful white light everywhere, it is so beautiful.' She then slipped back into unconsciousness.

Betty and I discussed what her mother had said, and because of Betty's spiritual beliefs she accepted this quite openly and it gave her much peace and comfort. I said goodbye to Mavis and Betty, and although Mavis had not been responding for some time, she squeezed my hand. I felt it was her parting gift for me.

As I was leaving the room the oncologist entered the room with a very stern cold look on his face and stated to the family, 'Not long now, only a matter of hours.' He then turned to me and asked, 'What is that smell? What is her daughter doing?' I explained that I had just given Mavis and aromatic lavender massage as she had been having them on a regular basis and that her daughter Betty was praying for her mother. He laughed in my face, and told the family that touch and prayer are a useless, and a waste of time. I felt furious, degraded and insulted, and when I looked at the family's faces I nearly cried. All the feelings of peace and calmness and inner strength that they had mustered had been destroyed in just a few minutes. After spending an hour with the family reassuring them and comforting them, I left to go home.

When I returned to work after two days off, the unit manager said that the oncologist wanted to speak to me. 'Oh my goodness, now what?' I asked the manager what time Mavis had died, and she gave me the most beautiful smile and gestured for me to look up the hallway. There was the Queen Mother, on her walking frame, routine observations back to normal, skin colour normal, smiling from ear to ear. She was discharged that day and went home to live with her daughter for a further 18 months.

The oncologist asked, 'What did you do in that room? What happened? She should have died. I have never seen anything like it in my whole career.' I just smiled and said obviously it was not time for

Mavis to go, 'Perhaps it was divine intervention.'

Two weeks later the same oncologist asked me to massage three of his palliative care patients, telling their families, 'Oh yes, touch is very important, and feel free to pray.' I nursed Mavis at home, until her family made the extremely difficult decision that they could not cope with her dying at home and that she needed to be transferred into Palliative Care Unit. As she left for the last time I quietly whispered into her ear, "I love you, thank you for giving me the privilege of nursing you and being your friend. When you get to the unit, just let go. God is waiting."

Mavis had only been in the unit for a few hours when she died very peacefully surrounded by all those she loved, her daughter, grandchildren, and the occasional waft of lavender oil.

~

To one who has faith no explanation is necessary
To one without faith,
No explanation is possible.

Thomas Aquinas (1948)

~

34

Flo: Fish and Chips

Florence – (Flo) was 90 years of age, extremely frail and had been diagnosed with aggressive breast cancer which had metastasised throughout her body. Her prognosis was poor, she was dying. She had an amazing attitude to her life, and such trust in God and her faith. She expressed that she was ready to return home, to be reunited with her husband in Heaven. Each day she would recite a different passage from the bible to me, as she pondered on its meaning. Her knowledge of scripture was outstanding; she could quote any biblical passage in the whole text. Over her bed she had a small cross, which had been passed down through the generations. Flo also believed greatly in Angels and the extraordinary power of prayer to angels when one needed assistance. She shared with me the many wonderful mystical encounters throughout her life she believed that they were always watching over her.

~

When we ask our angels to pray for us, we can be sure we have friends in the highest places.

Eileen Elias Freeman

~

Flo's Son lived close by and would visit regularly. He was also in the public eye, so privacy was extremely important. From all accounts he and his wife and children had been extremely loving and supportive of Flo.

However, suddenly, without any explanation or warning they stopped coming to see her, continually making excuses and only occasionally calling on the phone – this broke Flo's heart.

To Flo her family were her life and she could not understand why they would not visit. To the outsider she was a beautiful old lady, full of love and compassion, but then one never really knows what occurs in family dynamics and who was I to judge.

Flo had spent her younger years as a Missionary in India, where she meet her husband of 60 years. So she had lived a life of service for others. Her old eyes lit up as she told me stories of her mission work overseas, and the love she had for the Indian people.

Each time I came to visit Flo her condition deteriorated. I continued to try to encourage her son to come and visit his mother, but to no avail. The strange thing was that each time I spoke to him I could sense the love he had for his mother, yet he would not come and see her. I kept praying that this would change.

One evening as we sat talking Flo quietly told me with assurance that she would be dying in three days and before she died she would love a feed of fish and chips. Not only that, they had to be wrapped in newspaper like they were many years ago when she was a girl.

The next evening I went to the fish and chips shop, ordered 2 fish, chips, and potatoe cakes. As I knew the shop owner I asked if he could please wrap them up in newspaper. Luckily, he had an old newspaper stored under the counter. He proudly wrapped the food, and handed me the parcel. Unbeknown to me he had added two more pieces of fish, and large serving of chips. No fish and chips would be complete without a bottle of soft drink.

When I arrived at the house, to my surprise Flo was sitting out of bed in favourite pink dressing gown, in her large arm chair, by the old fire place. With many instructions I filled the fire place with wood. The flames quickly igniting, the room filling with light and gentle warmth. The smell of burning red gum wood wafting through the house.

We sat together in front of the warm fire and shared fish and chips from out of the paper. As Flo glanced down onto the newspaper, there catching her eye was a picture of her son. She picked the paper up and began to read the article. Her old eyes, filling up with tears as she read. "I owe all my success to my Mother, the values she taught me, the moral, she spent her whole life helping others less fortunate, she is now dying of cancer. I cannot go and see her anymore as I cannot bare to say goodbye". We looked at each other in utter amazement. My, how God works in mysterious ways.

Flo asked me to hand her the phone, dialling her son's phone number. The phone went to message bank. Her message said. I cannot bare to say goodbye to you either son, so please come and see me and have fish and chips with me one last time. Twenty minutes later there was a knock at the door, and in entered her beloved son, tears streaming down his face. They embraced, I left the room, and went into the kitchen, only to be called back by Flo to come and eat my fish.

We all sat around the fireplace, eating our fish and chips, words were not needed, God had worked an amazing miracle here, in bringing mother and son together. On reflection even the fish and chip owner played his part by giving extra fish, how did he know that such a reunion would take place, a little nudge from heaven I feel.

Flo her son, daughter in law and two gorgeous grandchildren shared two wonderful days together, laughing reminiscing and expressing their love for one another, while also discussing the mysteries of life. She spoke of her faith in God, prayer and heaven. Naturally, loving friends the angels got a mention, Her Grandchildren, listened in wonder and awe as she shared with them her encounters with the heavenly beings. Describing their exquisite beauty to the children. The day was finished off with yet another family dinner of fish and chips. Although she was extremely weak, Flo still managed to eat a small piece of her fish. Stating to all that this was the last supper.

The next day as prophesied Flo's, condition deteriorated quickly — she was dying. Just before this beautiful old soul took her last breathe, her son, gently bent over kissed her on the cheek and said goodbye Mum see you in a while.

Quietly and without effort, surrounded by the love of her family, Flo left this physical world and embarked on a whole new Journey into Heaven, escorted by her friends the angels.

~

Make yourself familiar with angels, and behold them frequently in spirit; for without being seen, they are present with you.

St. Francis de Sales

35

Bob: Timing Is Everything

Bob was diagnosed with advanced bowel cancer with metastasis to his liver and various other organs. He was given palliation chemotherapy to try to assist with symptom control and pain management. After the last round of chemotherapy Bob decided that he had enough and that he wanted 'nature to take its course', as timing was everything in the cycle of life. A time to live, a time to die. He expressed no fear of dying, and it had only been through the past five years of cancer that he really learnt how to live and how to love. According to Bob, this illness had been one of the biggest lessons in life, and one which he hoped to pass onto others. Life was short; it was important to make the most of each day, to live as though it was your last, to love until it hurt, and to give until you have nothing left to give, and to serve God with all your heart, body and soul. Bob had a strong faith, he attended Mass as often as he could. When he was not well enough, his priest would bring Holy Communion to him. He believed in angels, and was adamant that when it was his time to 'go home', the angels would come and escort him to heaven.

Bob had been, and still was, a very clever man. He worked as a watchmaker for over 50 years. He collected antique watches and used the parts to make magnificent unique watches of all shapes and sizes, from fob watches to elegant ladies watches, to men's' designs, they were so beautifully crafted, each part joined to the next with much devotion.

Being a nurse, I always wore my fob watch as part of my uniform. One day when I was assisting Bob in the shower, my fob watch fell off into the water, and broke. Bob was most upset about this, but little did I know at that time that he had devised a plan to rectify this problem. That weekend Bob went home for leave with his beloved wife Gloria. They had been married for over 50 years. Bob and Gloria considered themselves soul mates; this appeared to be a very happy marriage. Over the weekend Bob spent a lot of time out in his work shed. This was a place where he felt at home; he had created so many watches there over the years, he had observed his children play from the same windows of the shed, and had enjoyed countless cups of warm cocoa from his wife as he worked into the small hours of the morning. He was surrounded by things that he loved, nothing much of value, just nuts and small screws, safety chains, glass watch covers, bands of gold and silver, a warm heater, and a radio playing gently in the background.

In his home, his pride and joy was a large grandfather clock, which he had fixed up practically from scratch and had taken him over a whole year to complete. The clock had belonged to his grandfather, so was very old. On the hour, every hour, it would give out a loud 'ding, ding'. In the beginning Gloria threatened to smash the clock as the constant chime annoyed her intensely. But Bob loved the clock and, in time, so did Gloria. After having a beautiful weekend at home with his wife, with a visit from his children and grandchildren, Bob returned to hospital, tired but very happy. His eyes sparkled with joy as he shared all that occurred on the weekend – from the family visits, to his wife, to time spent in his shed. His spirit was alive even though his earthly body was deteriorating.

Over the next week, Bob's health deteriorated rapidly. He was dying. He just wanted to celebrate one last birthday with his family. The day approached and Bob had such a beautiful birthday. Even though he was extremely weak, and was drifting in and out of consciousness, he appeared to be lucid for the times that mattered. The family spent many hours with Bob, laughing, reminiscing about old times, and surrounding him with love – real love that comes from the heart, which is pure, with no conditions. It was obvious to all the health care professionals who entered that room how much this man was loved by his family.

When Bob's family left to go and get a coffee, he asked for me to come in and sit with him for a while. During this time he was lucid and spoke of dying, God and heaven. He was hoping that his angel was getting ready as he felt that he would soon be going on his journey. But not quite yet as 'Timing is everything'.

Bob gestured for me to open his drawer; in it was a small box. 'This is for you dear', he said. When I opened the box, there was the most beautiful hand-made fob watch that I have ever seen. 'This is so that you will never lose time dear, as timing is everything. I have cleared it with the management for you to have, as I know nurses are not usually allowed to have gifts, but this is special.'

I was overcome and my eyes welled up with tears. As I embraced this dear old man, I could see that he too had tears in his eyes, tears of joy that once again his craftsmanship was appreciated and would be treasured.

Bob's wife stayed that night by his bedside. At exactly 11.30 p.m., Bob's own internal clock stopped beating and he drifted gently off with his beautiful angel to heaven. The next day Gloria phoned the ward to tell me that at exactly 11.30 p.m. the grandfather clock had also stopped. Bob had returned to heaven on the day that he was born.

Yes, dear Bob, 'timing is everything'.

~

You will find as you look back upon your life that the moments when you have truly lived are the moments when you have done things in the spirit of love.

Henry Drummond

36

Fred: Carry Me Home

Fred was a delightful 85 year old man who had served in the Second World War as an Officer. During his time of service Fred had both legs amputated below the knee due to gangrene from battle wounds. He had recently been diagnosed with metastatic bowel cancer which had an extremely poor prognosis.

Being a bilateral amputee and having cancer did not dampen this beautiful soul's amazing spirit and the mischievous jokes that he would take great delight in playing on the junior nurses. Fred would sit quietly in his wheelchair by the window with a brightly colored blanket carefully disguising his missing limbs waiting for his next victim, taking much delight in frightening the new graduate nurses, innocently asking *"Can you please get me slippers sweetheart?"* Roaring with laughter when the poor nurse removed the blanket to reveal two exposed limbs, he would then call out, *"Quick someone has stolen my legs!"* At times the young nurses' faces turned white.

On other occasions one would enter his room to find one of his prosthetic legs being used as a vase containing long stemmed roses or daffodils. He had the most wonderful sense of humour and was always the leader of any practical jokes within the ward.

Fred also had a tremendous faith, and it was this that he claimed saved his life when he thought it was over. One evening, as I sat quietly with Fred, he shared the most beautiful story with me – of the footprints in the sand. Fred expressed tearfully, that as he lay semi-conscious in the battlefield he realized that his legs had been badly injured in the attack, so he prayed to God pleading for help as he did not want to die, as he had a young wife and newborn to return to.

All the other diggers were nowhere to be seen, it was just him, lying in the sand, hearing the distant gunshots that echoed throughout the surrounding trees. He continued the story motioning for me to come closer, gesturing with his hands as if he was about to share an amazing secret with me – a sacred moment. "I remember looking up at the sky and seeing the most amazing stars, they were so bright, their light was beaming across the night sky like diamonds dancing gently reflecting onto the ocean. I was sure that I was going to die, as I could feel my body becoming cold and weaker, I had lost a lot of blood. I continued to pray, and then suddenly out of nowhere a man appeared in a white gown, he smiled at me with such love in his eyes. He knew my name and reached out to take my hand. I cannot walk, I have no legs," Fred said to the stranger. He then said to me "I will carry you, there only needs to be one set of footprints in the sand". "The next thing I knew I woke up in the military hospital. On enquiring, not one other person saw the man who brought me in – no-one. They all thought I was hallucinating due to the pain, but I know in my heart it was the Lord, and no-one can tell me any different."

For Fred's birthday I bought him a copy of *Footprints in the Sand*. It was only a small gift, but it gave him so much joy and comfort. He pinned it onto his wall above his bed.

Over the coming months Fred's health deteriorated. He was dying, He said that he was not frightened and radiated a sheer joy of returning "home". He said that he knew he would be "Carried to Heaven" by the Lord. I sat with Fred during the night as he spoke of seeing a brilliant white light – "heavenly", so bright. His poem still above his bed.

At 5 a.m. the next morning, the Lord came to escort Fred "home", his spirit soaring with the angles.

As I prepared to wash Fred for his final journey, I glanced down to his prosthetic legs which were by the bedside, and to my amazement the poem of *Footprints in the Sand* had fallen off the wall and landed ever so gently on top of one of his prosthetic legs. It was evident to me that, yes, dear Fred, you have been carried home.

Footprints In The Sand

One night I dreamed I was walking along the beach with
the Lord.
Many scenes from my life flashed across the sky.
In each scene I noticed footprints in the sand.
Sometimes there were two sets of footprints.
Other times there was one set of footprints.
This bothered me because I noticed that during the low
periods of my life.
When I was suffering from anguish, sorrow, or defeat,
I could see only one set of footprints.
So I said to the Lord, "You promised me, Lord,
That if I followed you, you would walk with me always.
But I noticed that during the most trying periods of my
life
There have only been one set of prints in the sand.
Why, when I have needed you most, you have not been
there for me?"
The Lord replied,
"The times when you have seen only one set of footprints
Is when I carried you".

Author unknown

37

A Candle in the darkness

A smile costs nothing but gives much. It enriches those who receive without making poorer those who give. It takes but a moment, but the memory of it sometimes lasts forever. None is so rich or mighty that he can get along without it and none is so poor that he cannot be made rich by it. Yet a smile cannot be bought, begged, borrowed, or stolen, for it is something that is of no value to anyone until it is given away. Some people are too tired to give you a smile. Give them one of yours, as none needs a smile so much as he who has no more to give.

Author Unknown

I have included this story as it is one about deep faith, in adversity, hope in a place where it is scarce, and kindness and love to a stranger.

To read about leprosy in a medical journal in Australia was one thing, but to actually spend time in a leprosy colony in Vellore, India, another.

Patients in Vellore suffered from Leprosy and as a result of the disease they had lost limbs, arms, legs, and some a mixture of both.

The long ward consisted of a large shed, with a tin roof. It was extremely hot inside and the ward had only mesh wire windows for ventilation. The beds were cast iron, with one blanket and small pillow. All that the patient owned was on a small table by their bedside. The conditions here were extremely poor – pain management practically non-existent, hygiene inadequate, and food was extremely scarce. Yet, these patients appeared to be happy. As we wandered through the ward, each patient I met greeted me with a warm smile, which reflected the spirit within. As I approached the last man, he sat patiently in a wheelchair, waiting to say hello. He introduced himself as 'Abha'. Once again, the smile, and sparkle of 'light' in his eyes, was one of joy and happiness, not pain and suffering as one would imagine. He had lost both of his legs because of the disease and all that remained were stumps above the knee. One hand had two fingers missing, and the left side of his nose was deformed. Yet, looking at this man, all I could see was this amazing human spirit. He had a real presence about him, serenity. I spent several hours with this beautiful old man as he proudly showed me the candle-making unit, which had been developed specifically for people with leprosy. The aim of the program that developed the unit was to train people in the art of candle making, so that the candles could be sent to Australia and sold through a charity. The handling of the warm wax also provided the much needed physiotherapy for patients trying to strengthen their hands. In one year alone 1200 hand-dipped candles had been made. After we left the program, Abha said to me, 'I want to show you something'. Around his neck he wore a small wooden cross, 'I am Christian' he stated with such pride, 'and I know that God is looking after me'. He then said, 'Do you know what my name means in Sanskrit? Splendour and light, and it is all around me.' Why was I not surprised from the moment we met. I knew that there was something special about this old soul, and he was the only patient who spoke clear English. 'Everyone had a purpose' he told me, 'even me. If it is only to make candles, then so be it, it is all part of God's plan'. He spoke openly about leprosy, but there was no anger, 'Better me than a small child', he humbly stated. 'The only thing I miss is not being touched, not even a hug. People get scared you know, that is only human'. With this his old eyes welled up with tears. At that moment I remembered what Mother Teresa had once said, *The worst kind of disease is not feeling loved.* It was like being nudged from heaven. With this in mind, I placed my arms around this old man and gave him a long hug. He cried with joy. I just knew that in my heart God wanted me to do this. I had no fear – what was there to fear when I was doing what was being asked of me?

I reluctantly left the colony for the day, promising that I would return in the morning to say goodbye before I left Vellore. As I approached Abha he proudly presented me with a small parcel wrapped in newspaper and in it was the most beautiful hand-dipped pink and purple candle, which he had made for me. How did he know that they were my favourite colours? I think that he to also had a little nudge from heaven. He had tears in his eyes as he quietly whispered to me "Let your light shine brightly for all the world to see.", as he hugged me with such affection. I found out that he had worked continually all night on that magnificent candle – I felt so touched and humbled. The next day when leaving India I was told that Abha had died in his sleep, his wooden cross clasped firmly in his hands, and a gentle smile on his face. There was no doubt that he had meet his creator.

~

"If light is in your heart you will find your way home".

Rumi

~

38

Herb: God Is Waiting for Me

Herbert (Herb) was 92 years of age, and was in the final stages of Alzheimer's disease. He lived in a specialised dementia unit and required full nursing assistance with all his daily care. He could still ambulate independently, but became disorientated to time, place and person. At 4 p.m. each day he also experienced 'sundowners' wanting to go home and becoming quite agitated at times. Many years ago he had his right arm amputated during the war, so tasks were even more difficult. He was a kind and gentle man, with piercing blue eyes, and when he smiled his whole face lit up – even the hardest hearts would melt.

As Herb's condition began to deteriorate I began to visit him on a regular basis. One day when I entered the unit he was waiting at the door for me. Placing his arm around me and giving me a hug, he was most intent of showing me something of importance in his bedroom.

When I entered the room, he escorted me around to his bed head, pointing out 'The Lord's Prayer', which he then began to recite. After this, he asked me 'Do you believe in angels?' 'Of course I do Herb.' 'Well', he said gently, 'Each night I have two angels come and visit me, and they are so beautiful.'

Never had I seen him Herb so alert, the haze of confusion was gone, he was completely lucid. 'What did they look like?' I quietly asked. 'Beautiful, so beautiful, and surrounded by a bright light, so piercing that it hurts my eyes, and they bring so much love to me.' I sat quietly waiting for him to tell me more. 'They are coming tonight to take me to heaven', he confidently stated. 'Are you frightened?'

I asked. 'No, of course not, it is so beautiful – I am going home at last.' I then said to Herb, 'I think that you have been shown a glimpse of heaven and all that awaits you there.' 'Yes, Yes', he said, 'God is waiting for me.'

Those were the last words that Herb uttered. Within a few minutes of this heavenly conversation, he became extremely confused and disorientated. He could not even put a sentence together, let alone have the conversation that we had shared. I believe that through the grace of God, Herb was given that time of clarity to share his experience, and to speak of returning home.

I feel that often residents with end-stage Alzheimer's disease, who are getting ready to die, are on a different spiritual level. As their cognition is so poor, the spirit is heightened and they become extremely sensitive to mystical phenomena.

I sat quietly with Herb until he became calm again. Before leaving, I said to one of the nurses that Herb has told me that he is going to die tonight and return home to heaven. To this she just rolled her eyes in disbelief. I said to her, 'Over the years of palliative care nursing I have learnt to really listen to what I am being told by residents, as very often they have a deep insight, into their own mortality.' Once again she rolled her eyes. The next day I received a phone call to say that Herb had died quietly in the night, with no fuss; he just slipped away with his beautiful angels.

~

To see an angel you must see another's soul.
To feel an angel you must touch another's heart.
To hear an angel you must listen to both.

Author unknown

~

39

Gus: I Lift Up My Arms

Throughout the years I have had the privilege of caring for many courageous and very special souls. People who have had amazing lives, full of service, compassion, courage and faith. Giuseppe, or "Gus" as he was known to us, was no exception. He was a delightful 83-year-old Italian gentleman, originally from Agira, a small town in Sicily. He was the eldest of four children.

At the age of 17, his path crossed with that of a beautiful young woman, who lived in the streets below his. He was mesmerised with her piercing blue eyes and fair hair, which she wore up or in long plaits. He commenced a courtship which eventually resulted in a union of marriage for 58 beautiful years.

Gus joined the army as a soldier at 18 years of age, serving in World War II as a private. During this five-year period, he only returned home twice to his beloved wife and country. During this horrific period he was a prisoner of war in Germany for 18 months where he was forced to dig trenches. When he was eventually rescued by the American forces he weighed only 37 kilograms.

Gus married his childhood sweetheart in 1947 and in 1948 their one child, a daughter, was born. Times were tough in Sicily, so Gus decided to start a new life in Australia. In 1953 he left his parents and family, his wife and daughter, and travelled on the ocean liner *Sydney* which took 24 days on the sea to reach Australia. He was joined later by both his wife and his daughter who also took this arduous trip across the ocean.

Gus was a man who had displayed tremendous courage,

determination and faith throughout his life with all its trials and tribulations. I could only imagine the hunger, suffering and pain that Gus endured as a prisoner of war. He obviously had an amazing strength of spirit and determination to survive, when the physical body was so weak, undernourished and exhausted.

My path first crossed with Gus a few months after he had been diagnosed with aggressive bowel cancer. There was an immediate connection and a beautiful bond quickly developed between patient and nurse. The same courageous spirit and steadfast faith that had sustained him throughout his life was once again was being relied upon during his courageous battle with cancer.

The first day that I went to see Gus, he reached out for my hand quietly saying to me, 'You have been sent from God, to care for me just like an angel.' I had said nothing, yet he intuitively knew that I was there to care for him when he was dying. At this stage there was no discussion of palliative care, and because of the family culture, this was a difficult subject to broach. The family and Gus were holding on to hope through their faith – hope of a cure, recovery, remission. But very slowly within the following few months the trajectory and intangibility of hope was changed to that of gentle acceptance and a different definition of hope – that of a peaceful death with no anxiety or pain, surrounded by those he loved, hope for his family when he had died, that they would be fine, and the hope that he would be escorted to heaven by his blessed Virgin Mary. As Emily Dickinson once wrote:

~

Hope is the thing with feathers,
That perches in the soul,
And sings the tune – without the words,
And never stops at all.

Emily Dickinson (1830 – 1886)

~

Gus's prognosis was poor – he was dying. He wished to die at home with his family around him. Gus had a beautiful immediate and extended family, who loved him dearly, not only sharing his deep faith, but they were also devoted to his care.

As his condition deteriorated, Gus experienced many spiritual experiences, from seeing the brilliant white light, which he claimed to be so bright that it hurt his eyes – 'It was everywhere, so beautiful' – to the mysticism of angels, too glorious to describe standing in the corner of his room. Each night leading up to Gus's death, the angels were present, watching over him, giving him comfort and love. He also related having visions of his parents on a number of occasions, and was quite excited at the possibility of a reunion in heaven. He also expressed that for two nights he had dreamt that he was having a joyous party – with Jesus and the Virgin Mary, his parents and people that he had not seen for many years all being present. There was wonderful music and food: 'It was a true celebration' he stated with much joy.

That evening, although extremely weak, Gus insisted on joining his family at the dinner table for what would be their last meal together. Not that he was able to eat much, but he did enjoy a small amount of pasta, and a sip of wine. He sat at the table in his dressing gown, proudly wearing his beret which displayed various medals on it from the war. It was as though, once again, he was getting ready to go on a mission – but alas one that he had to face alone.

One day while the family were having a quiet rest, I sat with Gus, holding his hand, and very quietly I began to sing to him *Here I am Lord*, unaware that the family could hear me. This was a very special moment between the two of us; he responded with 'I lift up my arms to Our Lady'. This frail old man who was so weak, lifted his arms into the air as if to embrace a long lost friend. He stated with joy that Our Lady was present. I could not help but notice the most beautiful aroma of roses which filled the room, yet there were no roses in the house. Before his family came back into the bedroom, Gus looked at me with tears in his eyes, and made me promise that I would be there to care for his family when he died. I explained to Gus that sometimes God has other ideas, but I would do everything humanly possible to honour his request and leave the rest up to God. He seemed relieved as he was extremely worried about the impact that his death would have on his family, and how they would cope with such an event. Gus spoke continually of how blessed he had been with his marvellous family, his wonderful wife, and beautiful daughter, grandchildren, their spouses and his great-granddaughter. All this time there was still the most amazing fragrance of roses in the bedroom, just gently wafting past.

It was not long until his family came into the room; they too were astounded by the beautiful perfume, immediately accepting these phenomena as a visit from their much loved Virgin Mary.

That night after praying for Gus, when I went to sleep I had the most vivid dream. In the dream Gus told me quite clearly to rest peacefully, but to make sure that I came to see him before 11.30 a.m. as Our Lady was coming to take him home to heaven.

The next morning I left immediately to go to his home. His family were amazed as they were just about to phone me as Gus' condition had deteriorated, and he was now unconscious. As I approached Gus, I kissed him on the cheek, and gently whispered in his ear to 'Go to Our Lady, reach up she is waiting', and even though he was unconscious, he gently squeezed my hand. I said, 'I am here now. Here I am', without even thinking of the impact of the words that I had just uttered. I sat quietly as his beautiful family said the Holy Rosary for the last time. At 11.30 a.m. exactly, Our Lady reached down from heaven and gently, without effort, escorted her beloved Giuseppe home. Once again the room was full of the most beautiful fragrance of roses.

40

Pete: An Inner Knowing

I first met Pete while I was working in a Melbourne-based hospital as a graduate nurse. His story is one which will stay with me always.

Pete was 65 years of age, and was diagnosed with liver cancer with bony metastases and various other organ involvement. He was in and out of hospital continually for treatments. He had a large supportive and loving family who would visit daily; they were the light in his life. Before becoming ill, Pete had worked as a teacher in a secondary school, which he loved, he taught English and maths.

Pete was raised Anglican, but did not practise his faith – well, that is what he said. Pete's spirituality, as expressed by him, was reflected in his love of his family – 'That is what makes my spirit alive', he often told me. Another passion that Pete had was for music. He enjoyed all kinds, from contemporary, to classical, to rock and roll.

One morning, when entering Pete's room to give him a sponge, I clearly felt a distinct change of energy in the room, my intuition telling me that something was not right. I had only just started Pete's wash when he glanced up at me with tears in his eyes, and said, 'I think that I am going to die, very soon.' When I explored this further with Pete, he indicated that he thought he would die during the coming week. Although there was no indication from the medical staff that this would eventuate, my experience over the years, combined with my intuition, tends to listen to the patient rather than the medical 'experts'. So many patients over the years have had such a deep insight into the timing of their own death – it is as if God gives them a little glimpse of heaven, and the magnificence of what awaits them.

Pete had no anxiety about dying, he was tired and was ready to go; he just wanted to wait for his daughter to return home from England, and to meet his granddaughter for the first time. Pete's daughter was due to come back to Australia in the next month, but when he said this to me he had a sense of urgency to get her back to Australia as soon as possible, and once again my intuition agreeing with him.

As a graduate nurse I had to approach the unit manager and senior oncologist with the request to get Pete's daughter on a mercy flight back to Australia from England. I explained my reasons behind this request, and they just glared at one another as if to say, 'What does this Graduate nurse know? We are the experts.' But my intuition, combined with Pete's inner knowing of his own death, gave me the confidence and determination to fight for this. Combined with the pleas of his family, the medical staff finally yielded to me and the family and requested a mercy flight for the daughter to come home to Australia, even though the oncologist and unit manager felt it was too premature.

I was present when Pete's daughter, son-in-law and little granddaughter entered the room. It was as if time stood still, and Pete could not say a word; all he could do was to cry, his eyes and facial expression showing pure joy. 'Thank you God, you really are there', he announced for all to hear. This man's spirit was once again alive, and his faith in God restored in that instant. All that mattered to him was in that room – his wife, children, and grandchildren. As I left the room, I felt privileged to be part of that magical moment.

That afternoon Pete went home on overnight leave, even though the medical team were not enthusiastic for him to do so. He had a wonderful day with his family, filled with love, joy, laughter and music (as later was expressed by his wife). That night Pete died peacefully in his own bed, next to his wife of 40 years.

~

We are not victims of aging, sickness and death.
These are part of scenery not the seer, who is immune to any form
of change.
This is the spirit, the expression of external being.

Deepak Chopra

~

41

Agnes: A Chocolate Milkshake

This story occurred while I was working as a unit manager at a special dementia unit in Melbourne. I had worked there full-time for over 5 years, so had developed special relationships with both the residents and their families. Here I encountered faiths and spiritual beliefs and customs of all descriptions.

There was one little lady whose faith in God stays clearly in my mind. When I think of her, I cannot help but smile to myself as she had a most wonderful sense of humour, and was quiet mischievous. Agnes, a small 90-year-old lady, with pure white hair, blue piercing eyes and an infectious laugh, had lived in the facility for four years. She was diagnosed with Alzheimer's disease during this time and required full-time care.

Agnes had a wonderful faith and a deep devotion to Jesus, whom she would speak to daily. She would also continually speak to the angels, and would spend hours sharing with other residents how magnificent they were, often finding it difficult to articulate words strong enough to express their beauty. Each night, Agnes prayed and gave thanks to the angels; it was really beautiful to witness.

~

Make friends with the angels.

St Augustine

~

This beautiful old lady had complete trust and faith in God, and even at 90 years of age would kneel at the end of her bed to pray. Once when I asked Agnes how often she sees the angels, she simply replied, 'They are always here darling'. Agnes would go to the chapel daily to pray with a few other residents. One day, after returning from the service, she looked directly into my eyes and very calmly stated with much conviction that Jesus would soon be coming to get her – at exactly 12 midday – and before he did she would love a chocolate milkshake. I immediately made the chocolate milkshake which she drank with delight, her eyes sparkling with joy. Once again she enquired 'What is the time dear? '11.40 a.m.' 'Perhaps, I could have another milkshake before I go', she asked, much like a child asking their mother for a special treat; she had a cheeky glimpse in her eyes hoping that I would grant her wish.

Naturally I made another one, with two scoops of ice cream, which she devoured. 'That was wonderful dear, God bless you always.' Ten minutes later, at exactly 12 midday, this beautiful little lady died in my arms after collapsing onto the floor due to a burst aneurysm.

Although this was probably the most difficult death for one to witness because of the large volume of blood, it was also strangely peaceful. On reflection, I feel the peace was due to her tremendous faith, and her insight into her own death.

~

When someone dies,
An angel is there to meet them at the gates of heaven
To let them know that their life has just begun.

Author unknown

~

42

Ahsan: There But for the Grace of God Go I

Madras, India. People were everywhere, on every corner of the street, just lying there, in the gutter, or on a small blanket if they were lucky. One small family was living on a square of concrete, with a wooden wagon; this was their home; all that they owned in the world was in that wagon. They were so poor, yet had this tremendous spirit, about them. When I approached them, their whole faces lit up with sheer joy. 'Namaste', husband, wife and child said to me, hands gently clasped together. They were offering me blessings, yet they were poverty-stricken. I felt humbled.

The people in India have no idea of space as they all clutter around you as close as they can get. As we continued to walk down the street, more and more people approached us, following every movement with curiosity in their eyes. It became increasingly common to see little children begging in the street with their hands raised and their eyes full of hope – such little ones, begging in order to survive in the harsh streets of Madras.

After exploring the streets for some time, later that evening we attended an open door church. The church was magnificent, and full of gold relics, while the altar housed a statue of Jesus and the Virgin Mary, and above them was a gold crucifix. I found it difficult to accept the richness of the building, when just outside people were living and dying in the streets.

The music started and the choir began to sing *What a friend we have in Jesus*. After the service, which I had found a bit overwhelming due to the richness within the church, I left my friends to obtain some fresh air.

I wandered out to the entrance of the church, and as the light hit the stained glass window I noticed a figure just lying in the gutter. As I approached the figure, it appeared lifeless; my heart was pounding as I was sure that he was not alive. To my relief, as I bent over to gently speak to the man, he answered, raising his head, which had been cradled in his old hands. Not only was he alive, but he also spoke very clear English. His name was Ahsan (which translated means 'mercy'). He was 92 years of age, and had travelled for days to reach the church as he wanted to have Holy Communion once more before he died. Around his neck was a small wooden cross, which he proudly showed me. He was Christian. It was obvious to me that he was dying.

I went back into the church and approached the priest, asking him what others thought would be impossible. 'May I please bring Ahsan in off the streets, and into the church, so that he can receive Holy Communion and not die alone? His name means "mercy" so please can we show some?' Two men carried his frail body into the church, and placed him on the altar, under the large gold cross. I requested some warm water and towels, and after removing his soiled and tattered clothes, I gently washed his old body. A few minutes later one of the men returned with a clean dhoti kurta for him to wear. This consisted of a piece of white cloth which was then wrapped around Ahsan's legs and tucked into his waist to form pants. To go with this was a loose fitting shirt called a 'kurta'. As he lay there, clean and with dignity in new fresh clothes, it was difficult to believe that the old man before me was the same man who was lying alone out in the gutter only 20 minutes ago.

Ahsan was then given Holy Communion from the priest and the priest administered the last rites. It was a beautiful sight to witness. His frail body was supported by two strangers as he received Holy

Communion, yet he was so weak that he could hardly swallow the wine and bread.

His faith in God was amazing. For many years he had lived on the streets. He did not own any possessions; he was destitute and had spent most of his life begging to survive. But the one thing that he did have was his faith in God. It was this tremendous faith, which he had for years that had given him the will to continue to exist.

As I looked at him, I thought of Mother Teresa and her tireless work with the poor and destitute of Calcutta. At last I really understood the strength of the human spirit ... to look beyond the disease, the poverty, the brokenness, and see the spirit. *'The most important thing in life is to give a large part of one's self to others.'* (Pierre Teilhard de Chardin).

My mind quietly wandered back to Harry, a man whom I had previously nursed in Australia before I came to India. Harry did not want for anything – materially anyway. He was a millionaire who lived in a penthouse in an elite part of Melbourne. He owned properties throughout the world, several cars, and shares in various companies. Making money had been all that was important to Harry for his whole life. He was so busy being 'successful', that he forgot how to love – how to give love and how to receive love. He also had no faith or belief system of any kind – not in religion anyway; his faith was in money and shares, something tangible. But now he was dying, and was all alone. His only friends were his butler and maid; there was no family.

Which man was the wealthier – to be rich in materialism, or in spirit? I pondered on this question as I sat next to Ahsan holding his hand as he took his last breath. To me the answer was quite simple – it was Ahsan. Although he was a beggar in the street, extremely poor, and had no worldly possessions, except for his small cross, he possessed the three things that Harry never really found, that of faith, spirit and love, even if it was just from strangers. But one cannot really judge, as it is only there but by the Grace of God go I.

~

Any who is to find Christ must first find the church.
How could anyone know where Christ is and what faith is in him
unless he knew where his believers are.

Martin Luther

~

43

Sister Mary: Brides of Christ

The wedding had eventually arrived. All the residents were dressed beautifully in their best clothes, hair and make-up complete for all the ladies, and suits and ties for all the men. Everyone looked so smartly dressed, faces glowing with excitement.

The day room was carefully set up like a reception – tables all draped in white lace cloths, yellow roses on the tables accompanied with name cards, champagne glasses and, of course, a magnificent wedding cake.

The anticipation within the facility was electric and the excitement was contagious. The long awaited event was finally here. The aim of the day had been to create an activity where all the residents could reminisce about their wedding day, by being involved in another mock wedding. Even the nuns could reminisce about the day that they became Brides of Christ.

For one particular Nun, Sister Mary, this day held significant meaning, as it was exactly eighty years since she first entered the convent. She spoke with much joy and love about her life in serving Jesus and the Virgin Mary. She reminisced fondly about the glorious white veil she wore when she became a Bride of Christ at a very young age. As Sister Mary continued to share her story of her life, she played continuously with her gold wedding band, turning it with anticipation, almost like she was waiting to go somewhere and was getting impatient. Her life was fulfilled, she expressed no regrets, and felt that all was in order. With tears in her eyes she said lovingly, 'I long to go home. I would like to go tonight, as it is my anniversary, and I think one should return home on the day that they first entered the life.' She was so frail and tired, hardly eating and finding everyday living such an effort, yet she was thrilled to be part of the day.

The staff were all involved in various roles, from the blushing bride, and handsome groom, the bridesmaids, even the Salvation Army band played the music. All the residents' families had roles to play, one making the wedding cake, another giving the speeches and assisting with the wedding banquet. Happiness radiated throughout the room, while the sound of continuous laughter echoed throughout the facility. Eyes that were once distant and despondent lit up again with pure joy – the spirit was alive. Even those residents who would not usually respond were found to be humming quietly to the music. Others enjoyed a slow dance. The highlight of the day was when residents threw hands full of brightly coloured confetti at the bride and groom, it went everywhere and would be found in various nooks and crannies for the next two weeks.

After a wonderful day, all went to bed tired but still chatting about the day's events. That night when I went to say goodnight to Sister Mary she asked me to read to her from her Bible, John 14.2, which was one of her favourite readings: *In my Father's house there are many dwellings, if there were not would I have told you that I am going to prepare a place for you?* Yes, that is correct, the Lord is preparing a place for me right now', she calmly stated, reaching for my hand. She then thanked me for all my care and love over the years, placing her arms around me as she gave me a loving hug and kiss on the cheek. She then looked straight into my eyes and stated with conviction she would not be here in the morning, but resting in the palm of God's hand in heaven. As I left the room, she looked so peaceful, rosary beads clutched gently in her old hands, Bible by her side, quietly reciting the rosary. Sure enough, Sister Mary died four hours later on her 80th anniversary of becoming a Bride of Christ.

Let Us Be Radiant Brides for Our Lord

Father, like any bride, we are looking forward to meeting our Groom. Give us the grace to keep ourselves shining like stars in the universe and radiant as we look to you.

Amen

Psalm 34:5

44

Pa: The Circle of Love

Eric Percival Harmer was known to me as 'Pa'. Like my grandmothers, Pa and I shared a very special relationship. In his eyes I could do no wrong, and I just adored him. A solid man, slightly bald, with his shirt underneath always displaying his white singlet, he would spend countless hours out in his shed making the most beautiful wooden furniture.

He was the epitome of a grandfather – kind and loving, always interested in what was happening in my life, and willing to lend a hand and some wisdom when it was required. His life had been of service and he had experienced a rich tapestry of experiences.

Pa was born and lived the first years of his life in St. Kilda. Leaving school early, he worked for some time in an orchard. He then undertook the trade of shop fitter – hence his love of creating furniture. Pa and Nan married in 1924 at Holy Trinity church in Balaclava. They lived in Eltham from 1932. The house that they bought then was only 10 shillings, for a double block, and a 'shack'.

Nan would share with me the many stories of how they would collect fresh water from a pipe outlet nearby and use candles and kerosene for lamps for light. The bush track to their home was full of swaggies' tents.

Pa was the shire president of Eltham four times during his 12 years as a local councillor. He believed that a collar and tie made all the difference to his presentation as a councillor, but he hated to wear them. He was often known to take his suit to work and get others to cover for him so he could sneak off to meet others for community business.

Being the shire president gave Nan and Pa wonderful opportunities to attend lavish and grandiose functions – two were the Lord Mayor's garden party, and the visit of the Duke of Edinburgh, and the Queen Mother and Princess Alexandra. I still have the beautiful evening gown which my Nan wore when she met the Queen Mother. It is pink satin chiffon, with a glorious pink satin bow lined with diamantes.

Nan held dear to her an old exercise book, which was packed full of a collection of cuttings from the local press during Pa's time as a Councillor; they dated back to 1950s. This book contained all Pa's thoughts and ideas, which were carefully written in blue biro, with important facts underlined or highlighted. 'Now we are in for three years ... wonder what that will bring forth?' (From Pa's memories).

Pa spent innumerable hours out in his shed, where he created his beautiful pieces of hand-made furniture. He would use whatever wood he could get his hands on and create something beautiful; it would then be stained with brown varnish. He was also known for fixing things on the cheap; we would sometimes find a nail or piece of string in the strangest places.

To say that he had a sweet tooth would be an understatement. I remember as a young child going up to Nan and Pa's and Pa would give me 20 cents, which seemed to me a huge amount of money, to go up to the local milk bar to buy some lollies. However, when I returned it was he who ate them all! The family tradition of leaving two jelly beans on the kitchen shelf for my brother and I each time that we came to visit continued right up until I was 16 years of age. The jelly beans then were replaced by Freddo frogs.

Pa was always on for a chat, it did not really matter who was around; he talked to everyone in the district. He had a good personality, and was liked throughout the area.

Christmas time was a special time for him as he loved to decorate the tree, which was silver. The tree would stand outside on the front veranda, all covered in tinsel of various colours, fairy lights, and small metal birds of all colours with glorious tinsel tails. He loved to throw a Christmas party out on his front garden and would ask the neighbours. For the children he would arrange 'Punch and Judy' puppet shows, which was magical.

As Pa became older he started to experience frequent 'mini strokes' and often needed hospital stays. Fortunately he had little ill effect from the mini strokes until much later on in life.

Pa was a very good judge of character; he liked my fiancé at the time, but he was not convinced that I was doing the right thing. (Neither was I if I am to be completely honest.) The night after our engagement party, Pa had a massive stroke and was taken to hospital. At the same time my engagement ring cracked in half, – a solitaire diamond ring just cracked. A few days later, I called off my engagement as I knew in my heart that it was not meant to be. During this time we spent many hours in the hospital with Pa; he had become quite distressed, so they had bandaged up his old hands so that he did not hurt himself.

On reflection, 20 years later, I can see this as possibly spiritual distress or terminal restlessness. In those days, care of the spirit was not recognised as an imperative aspect of holistic palliative care.

We asked for the minister to come up and pray for Pa, as I could clearly see that he was very close to going on his journey. As we all held hands and prayed the Minister said, 'I have never felt such a circle of love in all my years of service.' My heart was breaking as Pa was the first of my beautiful grandparents to die, and I was very close to him.

I could clearly sense that it was just his physical tired old body that was struggling, and that his spirit was hovering between the physical and that of the next dimension. I also noticed that his skin that had been troublesome all his life with terrible psoriasis was now healed, with no scaling or bleeding; it was clear and soft. He was getting ready to go, all was in order. A few hours after this, Pa quietly died surrounded with the circle of love.

~

Will your soul be able to echo the words of the Apostle Paul, "I have fought the good fight? I have finished the race. I have kept the faith"? (Timothy 4:7-8)
Love is a circle ... the more you give, the more comes around.

Author unknown

~

Appendix A

Advice for Families and Caregivers

We come into the world by the remarkable passage of birth, and when our time is complete our soul leaves the tired body for another amazing journey back home to God – the Creator. This is the cycle of life, death, and life again.

In Hospice care health care professionals see death and dying as part of living – thus incorporating the philosophy of Dame Cicely Saunders, (1990).

~

" You matter because you are you,
You matter to the last moments of your life
And we will do all we can
Not only to help you die in peace,
But to Live until you Die".

~

Caring for the aged and dying is a privilege, as many healthcare professionals know. That is not true everywhere, however. In our society today, modern medicine is so intent on knowledge and technology about healing the physical body that it often overlooks or dismisses the human spirit.

Stories of blessings in the dying process show the amazing ways in which God touches the lives of both the patient and their family, regardless of their gender, culture, and spiritual beliefs. The result is often a strengthening of faith or courage for dying ones, and a sense of meaning and purpose to their lives.

As the physical body declines, I believe that the spiritual essence of the one who is dying is intensified, and it is during this period that those facing their journey home may experience mystical phenomena, such as visions of the Virgin Mary, Jesus, angels, amazing light, saints, departed loved ones and perfume. God appears to give each individual person a small preview of heaven, showing them what they need to witness at the exact time that it is needed, in order for them to die peacefully and without fear.

Whether you are a healthcare professional, a chaplain, a volunteer, a loved one, or a dear friend, by opening your heart to the supernatural wonders that you may experience while caring for the dying and their loved ones, you may become 'a little bridge to heaven'. Following are some suggestions for families and caregivers.

Fear Not

When entering the room of a Loved one who is facing end of life try to leave fear behind as Dying is a natural transition in the circle of life.

Do not be afraid to touch those who are dying, they are still the same person, the one who you love. The physical body is just shutting down, and is tired but the spirit is strong and awaiting its Journey home. By holding the dying person's hand, I believe this provides great comfort and security and conveys boundless love and compassion. Just as new born needs to be embraced and loved, those who are facing their final transition into spirit also need to be surrounded by Love.

When we are privileged to be part of the Journey with those who are dying we are often reminded of our own mortality. There are many questions which we may ponder. Who am I?, Why am I here? What gives my life purpose, What would I like to achieve before I die? What happens when we die? Is God real? There are also many emotions which accompany this process such as overwhelming sadness, fear, anxiety, panic, grief and loss of control just to name a few. But these to are normal and unfortunately emotions which families have to work though when a loved one dies. But know that you are not alone, that you have the support and compassion of the Doctors, Nurses, Chaplains, and the rest of the multidisciplinary team. But most importantly God is there with you, although you may not feel his presence, he is there, waiting patiently in the wings to escort your loved one home.

Prepare the Surroundings

When a Loved one is dying, it is imperative to create a calm, loving, and quiet space for both the person dying and their family. Just as the scene needs to be set for living it also needs to be set for Dying. There is no dress rehearsal in death and it needs to be done with Love, Peace and Dignity.

Families may help to create this sacred space for the dying by bringing in familiar items which give meaning and purpose to their loved ones life such as photos, a favourite blanket, pillow or doona, a soft toy, or even a visit from a family pet. All these items help to bring comfort and a sense of "Normality", to both patient and family. Each death is unique, so therefore each space needs to be individualised to represent the persons life and achievements.

Dimming the lights may also provide comfort for some people, but for others may cause distress and agitation. Families are best to take their cues from their loved ones, either verbally or non verbally. Such signs as facial grimacing, or general distress is usually a good indicator that lighting is to bright, and needs to be dimmed. But for some fear of the dark may also be problematic. The room temperature should be regulated according to your loved ones level of comfort.

For those who die in Hospice, the rooms are often painted in soft pastel colours to promote calmness and peace. Families are encouraged to bring in favourite music for their loved one to be played gently in the back ground. This may be of great comfort to the dying person and those around them. Music can also promote memories of happy times. In Hospice families are encouraged to participate in their loved ones care, as much as they feel comfortable to do so. Examples of this may include, giving a gentle hand massage, grooming the hair, spending time in prayer, reciting poetry, reading short stories, or simply just being present in that moment.

Even if one should die in hospital where there are added obstacles of noise, bright lights, machinery, bustle of people coming and going, with the right attitude and expertise of staff, the same sacred space can be created.

Hearing is the last sense to go, so continue to speak to your loved one, as I know through my experience that they can hear you. Reminisce about their life, adventures, fun times even. Your loved one may not be able to respond verbally, but often when a story is shared which has a happy memory you may notice a slight smile on your loved ones lips, or a blink of the eyes. In making the energy in the room as light as possible, it assists the resident to transcend surrounded by love.

Let the last thing that your loved one feels before they embark on their Journey is your Love.

From Your Loving Hands to God's Loving Embrace— Letting Go

Caring for a loved one during the last few weeks and days of life can be stressful and demanding period. Many different feelings and emotions may surface at this time. Carers and family members are often concerned that death will be a painful experience for the patient. However, the time before death is generally peaceful. There is a gentle winding down that may take several days. The body starts to "Let go", of life.

Over the years it has become extremely clear to me how important it is for families to be able to give permission to their loved one to "Let Go", and to surrender, This is such a powerful expression of faith and the last parting gift which you can give your family member.

Although this is extremely difficult and may cause pain and many tears, by surrendering your control and Trusting in Gods Love and Grace for your loved one it will also assist in their final transition. Tears are normal, do not hold them back, to cry is to express Love, and sadness.

This loving gesture also reassures the dying that you will be okay, all is in order, and releases them to "Go"., and that you trust and Faith in God, is steadfast. In return this will empower the dying to feel secure and confident in your Faith in God and his loving embrace which awaits them.

When a person is dying they need to know that those they leave behind will be alright, and will be able to cope, even though they will be extremely sad. Often this is expressed in a round about way such as :

"Do what you need to do", or "It is okay to let go". "I Love You", "I will miss your terribly, but will be ok".

Families do this in a variety of ways, such as holding of a hand, gentle wiping of a brow, or even curling up on the bed with their loved one and cradling the in their arms.

As a Palliative Care Nurse I have witnessed this repentantly. However, permission may need to be given often. This in return assist to relax the person who is dying, but they will not "let go" until the exact moment that God calls them home.

Through my experience it is evident to me, that the dying have this tremendous inner knowing of the precise timing of their own death. Countless times over the years residents have thanked me for my care, kissed me goodbye and told me with great confidence and without a doubt that they would be "Dying", that night. Sure enough they were accurate.

Love is one of the strongest emotions, we as human beings experience. I believe that in order for the spirit of the resident to commence on its final transition and to "let go", of the physical body, that it is imperative for family members to give permission for their loved one to go on their journey. How often I have witnessed residents holding on, for their families, struggling to grasp onto life, yet their spirit was ready to transcend into the light. Once permission is given, it is like an instant release. The person dying is reassured, that their family will be alright, and they let go, and their spirit is free to sour.

Touch

One of the most important gifts which we may give to another human being especially when dying is that of appropriate human touch. Giving gentle, compassionate touch to another human being is such an important gift in providing comfort security, trust and central communication. When touch is experienced as being caring and supportive by those dying it not only assists careers to develop a warm rapport with residents, but may also break down communication barriers, fear and promotes great empathy.

For centuries the use of touch through massage has been recognized for its therapeutic value. This modality dates back to Hippocrates in 400 BC as "Medicine being the art of rubbing"

Medicine was especially touch therapies, with the laying on of hands as the main form of healing. (Harding, 2005)

An important aspect of caring for a patient's spirit is creating the sacred secure space or opportunity for patients to discuss their fears and anxieties. Touch through the means of gentle comforting massage may provide the resident with the opportunity to experience an emotional release and sharing of concerns, which in turn have been linked to improvements of self-esteem and general wellbeing. Through a gentle holding touch which promotes relaxation, the resident is encouraged to feel secure, cared for, accepted, and nurtured.

Empathy and trust is also demonstrated by the health care professional, both verbally and non-verbally through the quality of the touch used and the "imaginative entering of the patient's subjective experience". (Kahn, 1997) This may be facilitated via the therapeutic use of silence, through relaxing music, or by the nurse using empathic listening, which allows the patient to "tell their story" and know that they have been heard and understood. (Van Ooijen & Charnock, 1994) Rogers (1980) agrees, claiming that empathy is about seeing the resident's world "as if it was your own", without ever losing the "as if" quality which related to an ability to understand to some degree in an emotional way what the person is feeling. In a study by Perry (1996), silence emerged repeatedly as an approach which was used by nurses creating opportunity for "listening and hearing", what was being expressed by the patient. As Mother Teresa of Calcutta states "We need silence in order to touch the soul of another". (Mother Teresa Personal Communication, Home for the Dying, Calcutta, 1980)

However, nurses and those caring for the dying need to be conscious that the experience of touch through massage or even gentle gestures such as a pat on the shoulder or holding of a hand is also very personal and may also vary depending on the gender, age, culture of the patient, the parts of the body being massaged, and how the message of touch is being interpreted.

In fact massage may be considered inappropriate or invasive to some patients and acceptance of touch by patients depends on a number of cultural rules, and personal characteristics. (Feltham, 1991)

However, when touch is accepted, it may provide healing, love, compassion, empathy, peace, and feeling of being wanted and cared for as well as assist in pain management.

When families witness that their loved one is cared for and can see the pure connection which nurses may have with the dying patient and the trust the patient places in the nurse I believe this assists to give the family comfort. The dying need to be touched need to be loved and need to know that they are not alone. In encouraging families to hold the hand of their loved one while as they are dying, and not to be afraid, it gives the person one last gift in enabling them to do this one final gesture of love for their family member.

We are born into the world surrounded by love, and being held, and touched by our mothers, and family, we should also depart the same way, feeling the unconditional love from those who we hold dear to us.

For Those Suffering with Dementia

Percy sits quietly in a wheel chair parked close to the nurses' station, many nurses pass by, but no one takes the time to speak. Mabel sits in a large arm chair in the day room surrounded by other residents, but there is no communication, she just sits staring out the window, perhaps reflecting on how her life used to be, reminiscing about her husband, children and the wonderful dances they would go to. In her imagination she see herself dancing, wearing her favorite purple dress, she smiles gently to herself, the spark momentarily returns into her eyes, her spirit nourished For these are the silent residents, the ones that often are neglected by Health Care Professionals, because they have dementia the inner essence is often forgotten, that of the human spirit.

Over the years it has become extremely evident to me that many residents with Dementia during end of life care may often develop a profound insight into the spiritual realms, God, Heaven, seeing loved ones, white light, visions of Saints and angles. In some way I believe, the darkness of dementia is lifted momentarily to give a period of clarity and it is during this interval that residents may share wonderful spiritual phenomena. I have witnessed amazing insight through the eyes of those with dementia – almost like residents have one foot here on earth and the other already in the next dimension perhaps, experiencing their own little glimpse of heaven.

Those with Dementia also often seem to have a tremendous inner "knowing" regarding the timing of their own death. It is important that nurse really "listen", to what the resident is expressing and just not to pass off conversations of spiritual phenomena as part of the dementia progression.

Prayer and Faith

Throughout the world a variety of people practice the
daily ritual of prayer to give comfort, hope and peace.
Prayers may be displayed in a number of ways, mediative,
contemplative, intercessory, conversational groups and
mysticism.

There are many definitions throughout the literature of prayers. Some authors describe prayer as the personal communication with one's God or higher power in one's belief system. While others echoes this claiming that prayer is every kind of inward communication with the higher power recognised as Divine – that is God. Dossey et al(2000). Prayer may be displayed in a variety of movements, gestures, and ecstatic outburst, according to the various forms of religious and culture occasions.

Prayer which is concerned with being quiet and contemplative is known as meditative prayer. Within Christianity, meditative prayer is described as time spent reflecting upon the divine, with the intent of achieving unified presence, where there is no separation, thus resting in the arms of God. Aldridge (2004)

It is essential that health care professionals respect and understand the imperative role which prayer may provide during end of life care. As the physical body declines and becomes weaker, the spirit is still able to express faith, through prayer and connect with God. This is the period where a residents Faith needs to be honored by all those concerned.

As a resident is dying I believe that, the human spirit receives tremendous comfort and peace in its beautiful connection to God through faith and prayer. I consider that, the sense of prayer and connection to God is often heightened during this transition period. This is made possible due to the pure willingness of the resident to experience God, prayer, Faith and surrender, while not having the need to explain or control the experience to family or Health Care professionals. As a result this provides a safe sacred place of openness, awareness and endless possibilities to other dimensions. Prayer is the one single expression which those dying are still in command of which may provide comfort, hope, love, courage, healing and faith.

Throughout my vast experience in caring for the dying, I have witnessed that residents who have possessed a "Faith", and were prayerful, have experienced a very peaceful transition, as fear was eliminated and replaced by peace. Prayer is not asking. Prayer is putting oneself in the hands of God, at His disposition, and listening to His voice in the depth of our hearts.

Mother Teresa (1980) personal communication.

When God Calls

When God gently taps us on the shoulder

We are called to answer the echo from within our soul.

We each have a unique purpose in life

Something which is part of Gods amazing life's plan.

When Gods gently whispers our name

We are called to step forward in Trust and Faith

Beyond comfort and security to move forward on our Journey

When God touches our hearts with his precious love

We are asked to become all that our Souls are destined to be.

Tracey Heath

Appendix B

Crabbit Old Woman

When an old lady died in the geriatric ward of a hospital in England, it appeared she had left nothing of value. However, when the nurses were packing up her possessions, they found a poem that she had written. The quality of the poem so impressed the staff that copies were distributed to all the nurses in the hospital.

This poem later appeared in the Christmas edition of *Beacon House News*, a magazine of the Northern Ireland Mental Health Association. This poem has since become extremely well known through aged care facilities in Australia. This was the lady's legacy for posterity.

What do you see nurse What do you see? What are you thinking When you look at me? A crabbit old woman, Not very wise, Uncertain of habit With faraway eyes.

Who dribbles her food and makes no reply; Then you say in a loud voice, 'I do wish you'd try'. Who seems not to notice the things that you do, And forever is losing a stocking or shoe. Unresisting or not, Lets you do as you will; With bathing or feeding, The long day to fills that what you're thinking, is that what you see? Then open your eyes nurse, You're not looking at me.

Author unknown

References

Abba Gold (1979) *I have a dream*. Greatest Hit Album. Track 7.

Ady, T. (17th Century) *A candle in the dark*. *The Quotable Angel*. A Treasury of Inspiring Quotations spanning the Ages. Edited by Lee Ann Chearney. John Wiley & Sons, Inc., N.Y. p. 76. p.142.

Alabama (1994) *Greatest Hits*. Vol 3. Sept.27. Track 11.

Angelou, M. (1928) American Poet. Think exist.com Retrieved, 13.05.2012.

Angelou, M. (1928) *Little Messengers of Hope*. Carolyn Shore Wright. Harvest House Publishers. Oregon. p.14.

"Angels are the gate keeper to the soul" Author unknown.

Armstrong, L. (1994) *Louis Armstrong all time greatest hits*. Track.16.

Aquinas, T. (1948) *Introduction to Saint Thomas Aquinas. Faith sayings by famous leaders*. amazing_faithsayings. Retrived Sat, August 6th, 2011.

A Smile. (1980) Personal communication, Mother Teresa, Kalighat. Mother Teresa's home for dying and destitute, Calcutta.

Bell, J. P. (2008) *Humor Foundation*. Clown Doctor. N.S.W. Personal Communication.

Blessed Mother Teresa (2003) *A little book of Blessed Mother Teresa of Calcutta*. Columbia Press. p.71.

Bronte, A. (1820-1849) *The Quotable Angel*. A Treasury of Inspiring Quotations spanning the Ages. Edited by Lee Ann Chearney. John Wiley & Sons, Inc., N.Y. p. 76.

Brown, L. (1992) *Live your dreams*. William Morrow Paperbacks. The Quotation page. Retrived Sun 14th, Feb, 2013.

Burroughs, J. (1837-1921) Finest Quotes.Com. Retrieved. Sunday 10.02.2013.

Campbell, H. (n.d.) *Little Messengers of Hope*. Carolyn Shores Wright. Harvest House Publishing, Oregon. p.7.

Carr, B. (1992) *The Best of my Roses*. Poems you will treasure.

Chaplin, C. (1889) *Laughter is the best medicine*. Compiled by Evelyn Beilenson & Lois Kaufman. Peter Pauper Press. New York. p.4.

Chopra, Deepak (n.d.) 1-Famous-Quotes.com Retrieved Sat. August 6, 2011.

Corinthians 1 (1996) *The Jerusalem Bible*, Popular Edition. Chapter 13: Verse 13. Doubleday. New York.

Crabbit Old Woman: This poem later appeared in the Christmas edition of *Beacon House News*, a magazine of the Northern Ireland Mental Health Association. This was the lady's bequest for posterity.

Cruz, C. (1989) *Prayers and heavenly promises*. Hail Mary. Familiar Catholic prayers. Tan Publishing. pp.114, 94.

Dickinson, E. (1830) *Little Messengers of Hope*. Carolyn Shores Wright. Harvest House Publishing, Oregon. p.25.

Downey, R. (2013) Executive Producer, *The Bible: The Epic Miniseries*. Lightworkers Media, California, USA.

Dyer, W. W. (2001) *There's a spiritual solution to every problem*. New York. Harper & Collins.

Ecclesiastes (1996) *The Jerusalem Bible*. Popular Edition. Chapter 3, Verse 1. Doubleday. New York. p.856.

Einstein, A. Brainy Quotes. Retrieved. Sat. August 6, 2011.

Elliot, T.S. Brainy Quotes Retrieved Sat. August 6, 2011.

Faber, F. Think exist.com. Retrieved, Sunday, 4th Feb.

Feltham, E. (1991) Therapeutic Touch and Massage. *Nursing Standards*, 5, pp. 26-28.

Freeman, E. E. (1994) Quoted in *The Angels' Little Instruction Book*.

Gibran, K. (1883-1897) *The Prophet*. A Timeless Masterpiece. Axiom Publishing.

Graham, B "Angels". Brainy Quotes. Retrieved, Sunday, 4th Feb, 2013.http://www.brainyquotes.com/quote/authors/b/billy/graham_4html

Harding, J. (2005) *Aromatherapy Massage For You. The practical step-by-step to Aromatherapy massage at home*, p. 34.

Harmer, O. (1983) Quote from personal Journal. Given with permission.

Hawthorne, N. (n.d.) *Joy a book of quotations to inspire and console.* Robert Frederick Ltd. England. Printed in India.

Human Nature (2001) *The Best of Human Nature.* People get ready. CD, Track 16.

Irish Blessing. Well known Catholic prayer. *Author Unknown.*

Jessye, E. (19th-20th Century) *The Quotable Angel.* A Treasury of Inspiring Quotations spanning the Ages. Edited by Lee Ann Chearney. John Wiley & Sons, Inc., N.Y. p.100.

John (1996) *The Jerusalem Bible.* Popular Edition. Chapter 14, Verse 2. Doubleday. New York. p.140.

Joseph, J. (1987) Warning. When I am an old woman I will wear purple. Papier-Mâché Press. USA. p.1. Permission obtained from Jenny Joseph.

Kahn, M. (1997) *Between therapist and client the new relationship.* W.H. Freeman, New York.

Kearney, M. (2000) *A place of healing : Working with suffering in living and dying.* Oxford University Press, London.

Keller, H. (1880-1968) Retrieved. Thursday, February 7, 2013.

King, M. L. Brainy Quotes. Retrieved. Thursday, February 7, 2013.

Kinkade, T. *The Quotable Angel.* A Treasury of Inspiring Quotations spanning the Ages. Edited by Lee Ann Chearney. John Wiley & Sons, Inc., N.Y. p.47.

Külber-Ross, E. (2006) "Soul Gifts in disguise", in Handbook for the soul. Vol. 9

Külber-Ross, E. (1926) as cited in Harman. J. (2008). *Renovate your life:* Every season of the year. Author House. Bloomington. IN. p.178.

"Love is a circle ...." Author Unknown.

Luke (1996) *The Jerusalem Bible.* Popular Edition. The Holy Rosary. Chapter 1, Verse 28. Doubleday. New York.

Lynn, V. (2009) We'll meet again – the very best of Vera Lynn. CD. Track 3.

McKenna. M. (2001) May you always have an angel by your side. A Blue mountain arts collection. Ed. Douglas Pagels. p.21.

Moody, D. L. *As cited in* Wright. C. (2009) *Little Messengers of Hope.* Carolyn Shores Wright. Harvest House Publishing, Oregon. p.51.

Mother Teresa (1980) Personal Communication. Home for the Dying and Destitute, Calcutta.

Niebuhr, R. (1986) The essential Reinhold Neibuhr. Selected essays and addresses. The Serenity Prayer. A view of life from the sidelines. Yale University. p. 251.

Nightingale, F. (1986) *Notes on Nursing: What it is and what it is not.* London, Harrison. p. 60.

Nurses Prayer. *Author Unknown.*

Pagels, D. (2001) *May you always have an Angel by your side.* Ed. Douglas Pagels. Blue Mountain press. Colorado. p.1.

Palliative Care Australia (2010) *Guidelines of a Palliative Approach in Residential Aged Care.* Enhanced Version - May 2006. Australian Government. Department of Health and Aging. p.1.

Perry, B. (1996) Influences of Nurse gender on the use of silence, touch and humour. *International Journal of Palliative Care* (2), pp. 7-14.

Philippians, (1984) *Holy Bible. New International Version (N.I.V.)* English Translation. Chapter 2, Verse 15.

Pierre Teilhard de Chardin (1955) *"Le Phénomène Humain"* (First Publication) English version *Phenomenon of Man.* Published. W. M. Collins Sons & Co. Ltd., London.

Pierre Teilhard de Chardin (n.d.) Retrieved. Tuesday 12th February, 2013.

Proverbs (1996) *The Jerusalem Bible*. Popular Edition. Chapter 17, Verse 22. Doubleday. New York. p.833.

Psalms (1984) *Holy Bible. New International Version (N.I.V.)*. English Translation.

Psalm 34.5.50

Rodgers, C.R. (1980) *A way of being*. Houngton, Mifflin, Boston MA.

Schweitzer, A. (n.d.) *The Beauty of Friendship*. Daily Quotes and Bible Verses. August 22nd 2012. Quote. Day Spring Publishing.

Shakespeare, W. (1564-1616) *A Midsummer's Night's Dream*. As cited in Jacobson, Karin. *Cliffs Notes on A Midsummer Night's Dream*. 9 Feb 2013. Scene two. Act 121.

Shakespeare, W. (1564-1616) *Merchant of Venice*. Boston. p.192.

Socrates (360 BC) *As cited in Plato*. The Republic. Book One. p.17.

St. Augustine (4th-5th century) *Early Christian Church Father & philosopher. The Quotable Angel*. A Treasury of Inspiring Quotations spanning the ages. Edited by Lee Ann Chearney. John Wiley & Sons, Inc., N.Y. p.4.

St. Francis de Sales (2007) May you always have an Angel by your side. Ed. Douglas Pagels. p.25.

St. Francis of Assisi (1912) *Lord make me an Instrument*. Catholic Christian Prayer. The Little Bell (First Publication).

St. Therese (1873-1897) *The Story of a Soul*. The Autobiography of St. Therese of Lisieux with additional writings and saying of Saint Therese. p.140.

The Clown's Prayer, Catholics online. Retrived 4th May, 2013, Author unknown.

Thoreau, H. D. *Little Messengers of Hope*. Edited by Lee Ann Chearney. John Wiley & Sons, Inc., N.Y. p.47.

The Soul. *Author Unknown*.

"To the world …." *Author Unknown*.

"To see an angel..." *Author Unknown.*

Vanbrugh, J. (Sir) *Laughter is the best medicine.* Compiled by Evelyn Beilenson & Lois Kaufman. Peter Pauper Press. New York. p.41.

Van Ooijen, E., Charnock, A. (1994) *Sexuality and patient care.* Chapman Hall, London.

Walker, M. (1987) *Beatitudes for the friends of the Aged.*

Warren, J. (2011) *Jim Warren Studios* (Permission obtained, 15.06.2011.)

Wharton, E. (1862-1937) *Spirituality & Alternative Healing Articles, Prose, Poems, Prayers, Quotes & Lyrics.* Internet Resources. http://skdesigns. com/internet/articles/quotes/wharton/

Wilberforce, W. (2008) *Inspiration for Barbour Publishing. USA.* O Christian. com. For the online Christian. Retrived, Sun 4th Feb, 2013.

Winner, S. (1868) "Whispering Hope". *Little Messengers of Hope.* Carolyn Shores Wright. Harvest House Publishing. p.13.

www.ingramcontent.com/pod-product-compliance
Lightning Source LLC
Chambersburg PA
CBHW062026270326
41929CB00014B/2339